Parenting a Child
with
Attention Deficit/
Hyperactivity Disorder

Parenting a Child
with
Attention Deficit/
Hyperactivity Disorder

by

Nancy S. Boyles, M.Ed.

and

Darlene Contadino, M.S.W.

LOWELL HOUSE

LOS ANGELES

CONTEMPORARY BOOKS

CHICAGO

Library of Congress Cataloging-in-Publication Data

Boyles, Nancy S.
  Parenting a child with Attention Deficit / Hyperactivity Disorder /
  Nancy S. Boyles and Darlene Contadino.
       p.   cm.
  Includes bibliographical references and index.
  ISBN 1-56565-446-3
  1. Attention-deficit hyperactivity disorder—Popular works.
  I. Contadino, Darlene. II. Title.
  RJ506.H9B69   1996
  649'.153—dc 20   96-921
                                                              CIP

Requests for such permissions should be addressed to:
Lowell House
2020 Avenue of the Stars, Suite 300
Los Angeles, CA 90067

Lowell House books can be purchased at special discounts when ordered in
bulk for premiums and special sales. Contact Department TC at the address
above.

Publisher: Jack Artenstein
Associate Publisher, Lowell House Adult: Bud Sperry
Managing Editor: Maria Magallanes
Text design: Mary Ballachino

Manufactured in the United States of America
10 9 8 7 6 5 4 3 2 1

To my husband and loving partner David, who once again freely gave his support and encouragement to another one of my "adventures" as I travel down the road of ADD. To my son Christian, thank you for allowing me to share personal triumphs and pains in hope that your experience might be a light shining in the darkness for parents and children struggling with their ADD.

—NSB

To the great FDB who taught me about strengths. To my family, especially my children, Nicole, Tim, and Tom, who continually dazzle me with their creativity.

—DBC

NOT I, NOT ANY ONE ELSE CAN TRAVEL THAT ROAD FOR YOU, YOU MUST TRAVEL IT FOR YOURSELF.
—Walt Whitman

Best wishes, good luck, and have fun as you travel the road of parenting a child with ADD.

—Nancy and Darlene

Acknowledgments

We would like to express our gratitude to all of the following individuals who helped make this publication possible.

Attorney Stuart A. Schloss, Jr., who assisted us in the contract negotiations. Judy Leonard-Case who is kind enough to contribute a letter to parents and who was one of the readers of the manuscript. Ruth Guentter, Kay Colbert, Frank Monaco, and Christian Boyles, who also contributed articles. Eileen Kjeldsen for her advise and review of the legal rights sections of the book. Susan Kerscher, speech pathologist, for her review of the language disorders section of the communication chapter. Rick Leffler for agreeing to be interviewed.

Barber Easter, Tina Conners, and Dave Hamilton for technical assistance.

Melvin D. Levine, M.D., for allowing us to use the medication chart and also for taking the time to review the manuscript. Arnold Shapiro, M.D., for updating the medication chart located in the appendix.

Paul Loechle and the teachers at St. Ursula Villa School for their patience, flexibility, and support of Nancy during the writing of the manuscript.

All the parents who have shared their experiences and helped us to learn.

Contents

List of Figures

Preface

"Write about what you know best. Write about your experiences and expertise." This is common advice given to anyone writing for an audience, whether it be a third grader or a renowned author. Heeding this advice we, Darlene Contadino and Nancy Boyles, have prepared a manual based on what we know best—day-to-day living as parents of children with attention-deficit disorders.

Both authors were introduced to the world of attention deficit disorders (ADD) at about the same time. Nancy's son, Christian, was diagnosed in 1987 at the age of fourteen. Darlene's sons, Tim and Tom, were diagnosed with ADD and learning disabilities at the ages of eleven and six. Neither author has ADD, but both of our spouses do, and the genetic thread is woven throughout both of our extended families.

At the time of the diagnoses, very little information and support was available to the general public. When Christian was diagnosed, Nancy attempted to find more literature to study and other parents to support her. Nothing was available. She felt isolated and alone. There was no one to talk to and no one's footprints to follow.

Professionally, Nancy also felt stranded. At the time Christian was diagnosed, she was a classroom teacher. Children who were struggling in her classroom were demonstrating characteristics somewhat similar to Christian's. In an attempt to gain support for these children, she turned to the school psychologist, only to find that after testing the children and finding that they did not qualify for services, the school could offer no further help. So professionally, she was on her own.

By using her experiences as a mother, Nancy began to find ways to help her students, but it took an enormous amount of self-talk and energy. Asking herself, "Now, when Christian did that, what worked?" She would then proceed to implement in the classroom the intervention she had tried successfully with Christian. Surprisingly, more often than not, it would work! However, everything was clearly trial and error.

When a student would misbehave or push her buttons, it was amazing how calm and rational Nancy could become by thinking as a parent. "Now, if Christian is doing this in his classroom"—and he probably was—"how would I want his teacher to handle it? How would this child's parent want me to handle this situation?" The constant change between walking in the teacher's shoes and those of the parent was the way she coped with the lack of information and training in how to meet the needs of her own son and her students. Little did she realize that this was her on-the-job training for the positions she now holds.

Because Nancy has been on both sides of the fence, she can understand the position of the parents of a child with ADD and the teacher who is attempting to educate that child. Both need support, and both need to support each other.

Darlene's introduction to ADD was more gradual. She has three children: Nicole, 24; Tim, 18; and Tommy, 16. When Nicole was five years old, she developed viral encephalitis. Her illness began with a simple headache, which the doctors attributed to a virus. Within two weeks she was having seizures, was rushed to the hospital, and lapsed into a coma. For five days she remained in a coma in intensive care. As she recovered, Darlene and her husband didn't know what to expect. Would her learning be impaired? Would she have a normal life?

When she began first grade that fall, they got their answers. Yes, her learning was affected, and yes, she had normal intelligence, and she would have a normal life. For the next two years, Nicole attended Springer School, a special school for children with learning disabilities. After specialized instruction and remediation, she returned to her home school and, with support, graduated from high school. Today she is married and has a beautiful baby boy.

When Tim entered school, Darlene was very sensitive to learning problems that could interfere with school success. After her experience with Nicole, she thought she knew what a learning problem looked like. Having no experience with a "normal learner"—whatever that is—she was not sure what to expect. Tim did not seem to have a problem learning. Sure, his handwriting resembled something from an ancient Egyptian tomb. But what the heck—Darlene's wasn't anything to brag about either. And after all, he was a lefty. Still, Tim never seemed to reach his potential. Many of his teachers thought he was lazy or unmotivated. Who knew?

It wasn't until Tommy arrived in the first grade that Darlene's eyes were opened. Tom was all boy. When he was in kindergarten, he got an "outstanding" in self-concept and a "needs to improve" in self-control. He often walked backward down the hall, banging his lunch box against lockers (it makes a great echo).

He knew things one day and didn't the next. "He's just immature," the teachers said. "He'll be better by the time he gets to first grade." Unfortunately, that didn't happen. In this more structured setting, he was more restricted and was often jumping out of his seat and never seemed to know what was going on in class or be able to follow simple directions. After three visits to the principal the first week of school (I'm not kidding here), Darlene knew they were in trouble and something had to be done. But she didn't know what.

Luckily, her pediatrician knew about ADD and suggested a complete educational evaluation to rule out learning disabilities. Darlene and her husband were surprised to learn their little dynamo had ADD with hyperactivity and learning disabilities. What the heck did that mean?

Now that she knew the why, she had to discover what to do. As Nancy said, there was very little knowledge and even less support available to us as parents when our children were first diagnosed. As Darlene learned more, it became apparent that Tim, her older son, was not really lazy or unmotivated. He just had ADD, with distractibility and inattention being his main symptoms. Now she was on a roll. She had evidence that her kids were OK. They might learn differently—but they could learn and learn pretty darn well too!

Unfortunately, her own knowledge did not bring immediate change. Appalled by the lack of knowledge about ADD in the school system and the stigma placed upon children who learn differently, Darlene joined with a friend and parent of a child with ADD, Judy Case, and a handful of parents in the Cincinnati area. They recognized a need to educate and support themselves, other parents, educators, and the medical and mental health communities. Out of this need, the Attention Deficit Disorder Council of Greater Cincinnati (ADDC) was born. Less than a decade later, this council is more than four hundred strong and a very influential presence in the community. Each year the ADDC hosts a major conference featuring leading researchers in the field of ADD as presenters. Attendance at these conferences ranges between seven hundred and a thousand people. Parents, educators, physicians, and mental health professionals sit together, side by side, and learn how to help each other and the children.

Although Darlene realized she could change many things as a parent in both her school and community, she felt she needed to become more educated and credentialed to really make a difference. In the fall of 1990, she decided to return to school. She graduated with a bachelor's degree in social work in 1995, and in June of 1996 she graduated with a master's in social work. Her undergraduate internship was at a drug and alcohol recovery center, where she worked with children and family members of substance abusers or chemically dependent individuals and did assessments and individual counseling with clients who were substance abusers. Her graduate internship was at the Veterans Hospital in Cincinnati, where she is currently employed as a social worker in the Substance Abuse Rehabilitation Program.

Nancy facilitates an intensive class on ADD offered each summer at the University of Cincinnati. It is designed to educate teachers and support personnel. It provides those attending with detailed information about ADD, gets their questions answered by professionals, and allows participants to share experiences and ideas and to leave at the end of the term with strategies and interventions they can take back to their schools and share.

Unfortunately, this is the only course on ADD offered through the university for educators. So during the school year, Nancy modifies the course she facilitates and takes the show on the road. As a consultant, she goes from school to school sharing information with teachers and giving them support. These are very short-term solutions and do not address the day-to-day struggles teachers encounter in the classroom.

To meet the daily needs of teachers and parents, Nancy works as a learning specialist at St. Ursula Villa School. It is one of the few schools in our area that has a position like hers. She provides services to the parents and teachers in the school. Her involvement with the students is very limited. It is Nancy's job to guide and support the adults so they can help the child succeed. Together they come up with the intervention plans of action defining everyone's supportive role.

With the staff, Nancy developed and implemented a program that has been overwhelmingly successful because it forms a partnership between the parents and teachers that she constantly nurtures. Professionals within the community and the school's reading specialist and speech pathologist help form a very effective collaborative team.

Darlene is also a part of the education process. She also does numerous workshops and community lectures and is a free-lance writer. As a social worker, she reaches another segment of society struggling with the ramifications of ADD. Working within the community as a health-care provider, she shares the knowledge and experiences she has gained as a wife and mother surviving the daily ups and downs of ADD.

This book is not based on theory or hearsay, but rather on more than twenty-three years of experience, both personal and professional. The pain, anxiety, and frustration you feel, we have felt, and still do. We do not claim to know everything, because we are still learning. Yet in every contact, we always learn something new and see another facet of ADD. For that reason, we are supplementing our information with a section called "Letters to Parents." These are articles written by individuals within our community willing to share the ideas and discoveries they have made along the road.

We have learned, however, that unless you have ADD or live with someone who does, it is very difficult to comprehend the powerful effects of this disorder. Our challenge is to help those without this point of reference see the disorder through the eyes of the individual with ADD. This challenge can become overwhelming as frustrations and lack of knowledge and training interfere.

Just the nature of the disorder complicates our efforts. Working with individuals with ADD can be a very humbling experience. Just when you think you have the disorder in hand and are beginning to make progress, something occurs to bring you back to ground zero. However, the ideas and strategies we offer in this manual are based on research, and we see them benefiting children every day. The interventions work, but it becomes your job as a parent to work with other professionals to find the right combination to help your child.

We begin by identifying and emphasizing the strengths of the children with whom we work. A child learning through his or her strengths becomes an adult succeeding in a career utilizing those same talents.

We have referred to our children throughout this book. We hope this helps you see the diverse manner in which ADD can be manifested. They have very different talents and very different areas of difficulty. This is what makes working or living with ADD so frustrating and fascinating.

In dealing with a disorder that too often focuses one's attention on the negative, coming from a strengths perspective can be a refreshing change of pace. It forces everyone involved, especially the child, to look at the positive. Throughout this book we place a strong emphasis on ADD being an asset rather than a liability. When a child's education is based on his strengths (yes, we know that schools are designed for those who are good at everything!), the foundation that will support him into adulthood is laid.

Collaborative partnership and the focus on strengths are the themes of this book. Together, they will help you guide your child down the highway of ADD.

Introduction

Parenting a child is like any adventure. It is filled with moments of ecstasy and fear. The outcome of this bold undertaking is based upon many unforeseen events and circumstances. One of those circumstances is discovering you are the parent of a child with attention deficit disorders. When you first learn that this little roadblock called ADD is part of your life, you may not be sure what it means or what to do. You might even doubt you have what it takes to successfully meet this challenge. Have faith! You are on the road to an extraordinary adventure. Your emotions will reach incredible highs and lows, and you will never be bored!

As you awaited the arrival of your child, you may have dreamed of snuggling that little bundle of joy in your arms, watching his or her first step, and sending him or her off to school with new clothes and hair neatly in place. Instead, you might have gotten a little squirmer who didn't sleep through the night until he or she was two, doesn't like socks, and moves like a whirlwind.

Dad may have dreamed of teaching his firstborn to catch a ball, or of running alongside that first two-wheel bike as his child precariously wobbled from side to side, fighting to maintain balance as Dad let go for moments at a time. Instead, you might have a ball player who prefers counting butterflies or studying anthills.

If you are reading this book, odds are you're not the parent of any ordinary Matt or Mindy. Your reactions to discovering your child has a disorder probably fell into one of two categories. You might be a parent who has always known your child came from a different mold and are happy to have your suspicions confirmed. You met the news with a "Hallelujah, we're not crazy!"

On the other hand, when you first discovered your child had ADD you might have felt like someone jumped you, kicked you in the stomach, and tossed you hog-tied down a deep ravine. You might be asking, Why me? Why my child? You might be fearful of your child's future. You might feel guilty. You might be looking for someone to blame, most likely your spouse's side of the family.

Whichever group you fall into, it's OK. Your dream has encountered a detour. With a little help, you can navigate this detour and get your adventure back on the road.

In this book, we will be your tour guide on the great adventure of parenting a child with ADD. We are on the road with you and share in the adventure. We are here to tell you that this bumpy road can be navigated safely and successfully.

We believe ADD is not a diagnosis of despair but an opportunity to discover all the wonderful ways your child can shine. Children with attention deficit disorders are like diamonds in the rough: It takes special care and time for them to dazzle. Our love and patience are the tools to accomplish this goal.

As you learn about ADD, you will see many symptoms described. You might be tempted to focus on all the negatives—all the things that are a problem for your child. Always keep in mind that navigating this adventure is not about discovering what is wrong with your child. Your child is not an ADD child. Your child is a multitalented human being with an attention deficit disorder.

The key to the success of children with ADD is uncovering all their strengths, everything that is right about them. These are are their tools for survival in our competitive world. These tools are the basis for problem-solving and bypass strategies and the armor protecting their spirit.

If you are lucky, you will not encounter anyone who thinks that breaking your strong-willed child's spirit is all you need to do to set him straight. These misinformed people do not understand ADD and are stuck on blaming and quick fixes.

Parents desperate to find relief often become victims of inaccurate information and unrealiable interventions. The best defense against false hope is to become educated. Reading journals, newsletters, and books about ADD, participating in local support groups, learning the laws protecting your child's rights, and attending meetings and workshops will keep you knowledgeable and up-to-date. Avoid seeking a quick fix. With ADD, there is no such thing. Like everything in life that is worthwhile, success for children with ADD requires some work to achieve.

Part 1 of this book is designed to give the basic information about attention deficit disorders. We have tried to keep the language simple so as not to overwhelm you. However, some of the technical jargon has been included. Knowing the correct terminology will allow you to feel more comfortable when you hear it used by professionals.

Woven throughout the basic information are strategies and ideas you may find useful when working with your child. These are interventions we have used successfully with our own children and the children with whom we work. We have provided only a limited number of strategies to give you a starting place for thinking of your own creative ideas that will help your child.

Finally, how successful your child is in life starts with how he feels in his heart. An inflated ego caused by an overabundance of success is not a problem too many children with ADD experience. Strive to teach your child self-control, not to control your child. Help your child harness his creativity, rather than smothering it. Build your child up by helping him learn to use his strengths to navigate around those roadblocks to success.

In the book *Hyperactive Children Grown Up* by Gabrielle Weiss and Lily Trokenberg Hechtman, young people were surveyed as part of a longitudinal study. They were asked what was most helpful to them in growing up with ADD. The answer was surprising: having one person who believed in them and was there to support them through the rough times. This person could have been a teacher, counselor, friend, or parent. Who will be that person for your child?

It's a scary thought. You might be the only person your child can turn to when the road gets bumpy and tough. Respect, protect, and treat your child with unconditional love and she will turn to you for guidance when the adventure gets rough. Judge, condemn, or withhold love from your child and she may have no one.

Children with attention deficit disorders are like the light under a bushel basket. So, Mom and Dad, be the one to lift up the basket and nourish the flame that is your child's heart and help your child to shine, shine, shine. Your child is waiting for you. Grab your navigational charts, gather your supplies, and get ready. Your adventure is beginning.

PART ONE

*Understanding and Managing
Attention Deficit Disorders*

1

What ADD Is All About

The Invisible Disorder

Julie, a fifth grader, stared in disbelief at the grade on a math test that had just been returned to her—98 percent. This was the highest grade she had received on a math test all year. Sixty-eights were closer to what she was used to receiving. She should have been elated. Instead she was close to tears.

"See what happens when you study!" her teacher commented as she handed Julie the test. "Keep up the good work!"

The pressure was on. Julie was caught between a rock and a hard place. She had always studied for her tests but had done poorly, nonetheless, so she did not know why she scored so high on this one. It was a fluke. It wasn't that she understood the material any better or had prepared any differently. Julie always tried to do her best and wished that all of her test scores could have been 98s.

So why didn't her teacher understand this? Instead of being proud of her accomplishment, all Julie could think about was the pressure this grade now placed on her. "Keep up the good work!" echoed in her head. She did not know what she had done to get that grade and was worried that if she did not repeat it on the next test, everyone would think she was lazy and not trying. Wondering what she should do, Julie reasoned she really must be stupid. What other explanation could there be?

This scenario is very characteristic of a disorder called attention deficit disorder, or ADD. It is often referred to as the invisible disorder. Individuals diagnosed with ADD have no physical reminders of their disorder. They are intelligent and creative, and they outwardly look like their peers. There are no hearing devices or wheelchairs to indicate a disability.

The difference is located within the brain. ADD is a neurological disorder. This is not to say that individuals with ADD are brain damaged or mentally deficient in any way. Rather, it means the brain sees the world through a different lens. Melvin Levine, M.D., Director of Clinical Center for Study of Development and Learning at the University of North Carolina, Chapel Hill, describes the brain as being "wired differently."

The inability to see the workings of the brain makes it difficult to remember a disability exists. This is why children with ADD are often labeled dumb, stupid, lazy, and unmotivated. As parents, we often hear that our children could do better if only they would try harder. The irony is that these children are already working much harder than their classmates without experiencing success for their efforts.

Because each brain is unique, ADD looks very different in each individual. No two individuals demonstrate the hallmark characteristics of inattention, hyperactivity, and impulsivity in exactly the same way. You don't even need to be hyperactive to have ADD. Some individuals are only inattentive, while others may be hyperactive and impulsive, or exhibit all three characteristics. That is why ADD has to be managed on an individual basis. What works for one person may not work for another. This variation adds to the complexity and mystery of the disorder.

Inconsistency is another facet of ADD. One minute the child may be working diligently, and the next, he's a million miles away. Your child may know every spelling word when practicing at home but frequently will fail the test at school, or, like Julie, have grades that peak at 98 and then sink into the depths of the 60s. If her grades were charted on a graph, they would look like a mountain range in a geography book.

Just when parents think they have the disorder under control, things begin to fall apart and they have to come up with a new plan. It is this inconsistency that drives everyone crazy and makes managing ADD very difficult. The consistent inconsistency is the only thing Dr. Levine says you can depend on when working with individuals who have ADD.

Without warning signs or physical indicators to alert the individual that changes are occurring within the brain, confusion can result. The actions and behaviors of the individual with ADD are often interpreted as stupidity, laziness, or a lack of cooperation or effort. The ease with which it can be forgotten that they are encountering mental obstacles makes this invisible disorder very challenging.

Many changes in how we view ADD have occurred just within the past five or six years. Until recently, the hallmark characteristics of ADD were often recognized but not understood. The explanations for why they were occurring changed from era to era. The following excursion through recorded research and literature shows how our understanding of the nature of ADD has evolved over the past several centuries.

Alphabet Soup: The Evolution of ADD

Attention deficit disorders have probably been around since the beginning of time. It is suspected that the creative genius of Mozart and daVinci was the result of ADD. The biographies of Einstein and Edison also cause one to wonder if they had ADD. Attention deficit disorders is not a curse but evidence of a creative, insightful nature through which great accomplishments are possible.

This disorder has had many different names over the past several hundred years. It has become an alphabet soup of terms, each reflecting a new idea about its causes. Interestingly, researchers' theories have bounced back and forth between biological causes and poor parenting.

As early as 1845, children with the characteristics of ADD appeared in literature. Hendrick Hoffman, a family physician, described fidgety Phil in his book *Moral Tales*. It seems Phil was a naughty, restless boy who grew steadily more rude and wild. The tale implied that Phil's parents were not doing a very good job of disciplining him.

In 1902, G. F. Still, M.D., looked at the characteristics of ADD a little differently. He was one of the earliest researchers to suggest that perhaps there was a biological reason for such children's behavior. He observed that the children's parents tried to discipline them without success. Dr. Still reported that the "defect in moral control" was a result not of poor parenting but of the child's nature.

This idea that the inattention, hyperactivity, and impulsivity were evident because of what was happening inside the body, rather than outside, was further strengthened after World War I. From 1917 to 1918 there was an encephalitis epidemic. This is a disease that affects the brain. Also, many of the doughboys returning home had received head injuries. Those who survived the epidemic and the head injuries were showing similar symptoms. They were overactive, impulsive, and less attentive. It was concluded these characteristics were a result of minimal brain damage.

Not until the 1950s and 1960s did researchers look more closely at the increasing population of children who demonstrated these same characteristics. The children had no medical history of disease, head injury, or trauma to the brain. It was concluded that they must have minimal brain dysfunction, or MBD, rather than minimal brain damage. Overly active children were diagnosed with "hyperkinetic reaction of childhood." It was reasoned that these behaviors must be a result of ineffective parenting skills. This was the era of numerous parenting programs to help parents "control" their children.

Criteria for the diagnosis of attention deficit disorder first appeared in 1980. The three hallmark characteristics of the disorder were identified as inattention, hyperactivity, and impulsivity. They were described in the *Diagnostic and Statistical Manual of Mental Disorders, Third Edition (DSM III)*. This is a manual published approximately every seven years by the American Psychiatric Association. It describes all the disorders psychiatrists diagnose and treat. Psychiatrists are medical doctors, and they make medical diagnoses and prescribe medications. Therefore, in 1980, the disorder became known as attention deficit disorder, or ADD, and again received a medical focus.

In 1987, the *DSM III* was revised and became the *DSM III R*. In this revision, fourteen characteristics were lumped together, and the name of the disorder was changed to Attention Deficit Hyperactivity Disorder (ADHD).

This change became very confusing. This terminology implied that in order to be diagnosed ADD, you had to be hyperactive. This is untrue. Hyperactivity is only one of the symptoms and does not have to be present for a diagnosis of ADD to be made. This change resulted in many misdiagnoses.

Females in particular were often misdiagnosed. Quiet and unassuming, seldom drawing attention to themselves, and learning early how to compensate to survive, females were overlooked and thought to be "spacey." Only within the past several years have physicians begun looking more closely at young females who do not seem to be progressing as they should to see if they show signs of ADD. This new focus is partly the result of the large numbers of females being diagnosed in adulthood.

The *DSM IV* was published in 1994. This is the edition currently being used by psychiatrists to diagnose for AD/HD (official *DSM IV* code). Although the disorder is still called attention deficit/hyperactivity disorder, the *DSM IV* now defines and separates the different types of the disorder. If only inattention is found, the diagnosis is "attention deficit/hyperactivity disorder, predominantly inattentive type." If impulsivity and/or hyperactivity is found, the diagnosis is "attention deficit/hyperactivity disorder, predominantly hyperactive-impulsive type." If all the characteristics are present, the diagnosis is "attention deficit/hyperactivity disorder, combined type (see Appendix A). These changes should eliminate much of the confusion presented by the *DSM III R*. (For simplicity, throughout this book, we will refer to this disorder as ADD unless we are discussing the hyperactivity/impulsivity factors.)

The *DSM IV* also states that these symptoms must be present no later than age seven and must be present in two or more situations. The symptoms often appear once the child enters school. The design of the typical classroom places a huge demand on the child's ability to pay attention, listen, and use self-control. Depending on the severity of the disorder, the organization of the classroom, the flexibility of the teacher, and the child's ability to adapt, symptoms may emerge in preschool or in later years. The transitional years of preschool, kindergarten, first grade, fourth grade, seventh grade, ninth grade, and entering college or the work force are the most critical times for individuals with ADD, because these are the years when academic and social requirements change.

None of the terms or conditions presented in the *DSM IV* perfectly capture the complexity of the disorder. As parents, we are often frightened and overwhelmed when we see or hear these terms for the first time. For this reason, becoming educated about the disorder is essential. Parents and caregivers, the child with the diagnosis, and the child's siblings need to understand how ADD is affecting them. *Demystification* is the term Dr. Levine uses to describe this process. It simply means "to remove the mystery." Once the mystery is gone, fear diminishes, and then everyone is ready to begin the task of managing the disorder.

Before we can discuss how to manage ADD, we need to be certain we have a basic understanding of the disability. Often ADD is only one of the disorders that physicians uncover. It is important to understand that ADD is rarely found alone and all the related disorders must be addressed.

The Who, What, and Why

By now you know the three hallmark characteristics of ADD are inattention, hyperactivity, and impulsivity. As discussed above, not all of these symptoms need to be present to receive a diagnosis of ADD.

Both genders are affected by ADD. In childhood, males tend to be diagnosed more often than females, but recent research studies indicate that adult females are being diagnosed as often as males. The ratio, once six males diagnosed for every female, is now one male for every female. This discrepancy has occurred because young males, more frequently having the hyperactivity and impulsivity components, tend to call attention to themselves, thus receiving an earlier diagnosis. Females, on the other hand, demonstrate the characteristics of ADD more subtly and are often overlooked until young womanhood. (Because both genders are equally affected, the pronouns *he* and *she* will be used interchangeably throughout this manuscript.)

Rarely is ADD found in isolation, making it a very complex disability. This is why it is now being referred to as attention deficit disorders. Dr. Thomas Brown, Ph.D., at Yale University, refers to ADD as the "wide umbrella" disorder. This means that individuals demonstrate ADD in a variety of different ways.

Often one or more other disorders are diagnosed along with ADD. Some of the related, or comorbid, disorders under this "wide umbrella" include learning disabilities, Tourette syndrome, language processing disabilities, sensory integration issues, obsessive-compulsive disorder (OCD), mood disorders, oppositional defiant disorder (ODD), and conduct disorder (CD). (See the Appendices B–E for *DSM IV* criteria on CD, ODD, OCD, and Tourette syndrome.)

The severity of the disorder depends on how many of the symptoms and related disorders are involved. A spectrum is used to show the intensity of the disability. A person mildly affected by ADD may have only the characteristics required to make the diagnosis and function with minimal impairment. Nancy's son, Christian, falls into this category. He is very impulsive! A more severely involved individual, placed at the high end of the spectrum, may show all three of the symptoms, as well as a combination of related disorders that significantly impair functioning. We know children with AD/HD, Tourette, learning disabilities, and a language processing disability all wrapped up in one body. School is excruciating for these children. Others, like Darlene's son Tom, fall within the moderate range. He has a learning disability along with AD/HD.

Figure 1-1
Spectrum of Attention Deficit Disorder

1	2	3	4	5	6	7	8	9	10
Mild					Moderate				Severe

Researchers are not sure what occurs within the brain to cause the characteristics of ADD. However, they do know that certain areas of the brain are involved and there is an interference in the production and release of the neurotransmitters. Neurotransmitters are the chemicals keeping the brain's communication system functioning. If the neurotransmitters are produced within the "normal" level, the individual functions consistently. When not enough of the chemicals are released, the inconsistencies occur.

Why this fluctuation in the production of the neurotransmitters occurs is still a mystery. The search continues for more definitive answers. Computer imaging of the brain has been helpful in revealing interesting and insightful information about the functioning of this complex organ.

Recent research by Alan Zametkin, M.D., at the National Institute of Health, indicates the brain's metabolism is lower in the brains of adults who were hyperactive as children. The metabolism is lower in the parts of their brain that regulate attention and motor control.

This finding substantiates the relationship between brain chemistry and performance.

Daniel Amen, M.D., is also exploring the functioning of the brain with the use of SPECT scans. In his book, *Images Into the Mind,* Dr. Amen refers to "hot spots" within different lobes of the brain. Problems in those areas result in certain behaviors. For example, a hot spot in the temporal lobe may result in aggression.

Many questions remain in the search to understand this complex disorder. Through the untiring efforts of researchers, we may someday soon have a better grasp on how the brain functions.

Until we know exactly how the brain is involved in ADD, it will serve our purposes to remember that it is an invisible disorder with no physical indications of an impairment. Because it is the flucuation of the neurotransmitters influencing the onset of ADD, the child's behavior is often misinterpreted. Therefore, it is very important for the parents to be able to recognize the symptoms of ADD and distinguish them from other behaviors.

It is also important to remember that ADD is not outgrown. The child with ADD will show the hallmark characteristics in any combination. However, the adolescent whose disorder has not been managed or even diagnosed will exhibit very different symptoms. Used to failure and frustration, by seventh grade the adolescent with ADD is often angry and aggressive and feels worthless and stupid. By adulthood, the feeling that he always gets the short end of the stick and nothing works out for him is common. Underlying anger and frustration make patience short.

Across the Life Span

"He's all boy!"

"Leave him alone. He'll outgrow it."

These are common misconceptions about ADD. A favorite statement made by fathers who later are also diagnosed with ADD is "Aw, he's just like I was when I was his age and I turned out fine!"

ADD is not outgrown. Until recently, it was commonly accepted that ADD disappeared in adolescence. Parents were often told to wait, and their child would outgrow the symptoms.

Today, many adults are being diagnosed with ADD. Thanks to the untiring efforts over the past several decades of researchers such as Paul Wender, M.D., Rachel Gittelman, Ph.D., Russell Barkley, Ph.D., and Gabrielle Weiss, M.D., we now know that ADD spans a lifetime.

The central nervous system of a child with ADD matures at a slower rate. This is one reason why the child appears to be less mature than his or her peers and often prefers to play with younger children. As the child ages and the central nervous system developes, many of the symptoms seem less severe. By late adolescence, the central nervous system has fully developed. This may be one reason why early researchers thought ADD was outgrown.

This disorder looks very different at each developmental stage. Pregnant women often can tell that the child they are carrying is a little different. Nancy remembers that when she was pregnant with Christian, she wondered how many babies she was carrying. She could have sworn there was a nightly football game going on in there!

After birth, the infant is usually more irritable, inactive, and requires less sleep than his counterparts. It was five years after the birth of Darlene's first son before she got a good night's sleep. Tim was two and a half before he slept through the night. Then she had Tom had to wait another two and a half years for him to have sweet dreams all night long.

As the child progresses into the toddler stage, he is often demanding and impulsive. He is prone to accidents as he climbs out of his crib to the top of the dresser. Toilet training is often difficult, and bedwetting is common.

As the child with ADD enters school, he is often socially, emotionally, and developmentally behind his peers. In childhood, the three hallmark characteristics, in any combination, are most apparent. Listening for long periods of time and following directions become overwhelming tasks. Keeping track of belongings and the need to be organized can be a monumental chore. Socially, the child with ADD often appears silly and disruptive. His impulsivity tends to get him into difficult situations where he loses control.

Education is the only area of our lives where, in order to succeed, we must be good at everything. Special skills and talents are rarely taken into consideration when curricula are designed. There is little room for specialization and individualism in the fast pace of daily routine. Therefore, long before many students leave elementary school, they have experienced repeated failure, frustration, and humiliation, and very little success.

Seventh grade appears to be a very critical year. Not only are students at the brink of adolescence, but also the demands of education change. Often the students leave elementary school and enter new surroundings with much older students. While adjusting to the new surroundings, they have seven or eight new faces making demands on them. The course work is more intense, and the pace is overwhelming. Students with poor organizational and study skills struggle to keep up.

In adolescence, ADD not diagnosed or properly managed begins to take on a different appearance. The hallmark characteristics become secondary to other issues. Hyperactivity diminishes while impulsivity may increase. Poor self-esteem, failure, and frustration put the ADD population at a higher risk for antisocial behavior, arrests, substance abuse, grade retention, and dropping out of school.

The cycle continues into adulthood. The hallmark symptoms underlie the inability to tolerate stress and mood swings. Maintaining relationships, holding jobs, completing tasks, and controlling the anger and frustration become difficult. By adulthood, hyperactivity has diminished, but many adults with ADD still find it hard to control their restlessness and relax. Completing tasks may be difficult, and pulling their lives together to achieve their goals can be a challenge. Figure 1-2 illustrates the transformation that occurs.

However, if a diagnosis has been made and a plan of action based on the strengths of the individual is put into place, success can be attained. The most effective approach is a support team, which might

Figure 1-2
ADD Through the Life Span

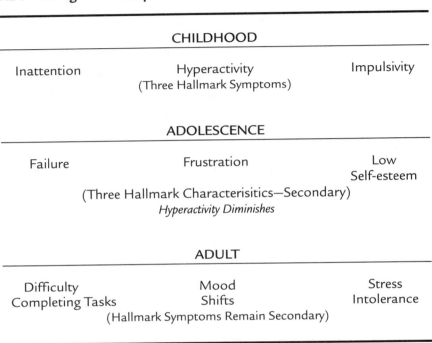

CHILDHOOD

Inattention	Hyperactivity	Impulsivity
	(Three Hallmark Symptoms)	

ADOLESCENCE

Failure	Frustration	Low Self-esteem

(Three Hallmark Characterisitics—Secondary)
Hyperactivity Diminishes

ADULT

Difficulty Completing Tasks	Mood Shifts	Stress Intolerance

(Hallmark Symptoms Remain Secondary)

include a physician to administer and monitor medication, and a psychologist or psychiatrist for individual and family therapy, if appropriate. Teachers and parents working with the principal, counselors, school psychologists, and the school nurse support the child during the school day. A speech and language pathologist, an occupational therapist, tutors, and social workers could also be part of the team. Everyone working together provides the support needed for success throughout the life span.

2

Getting a Diagnosis and Setting Up a Support System

With the frequent publicity ADD is receiving, calling it a mystery seems strange. It seems everywhere we turn we can access information about ADD. Many of the larger bookstores now have sections devoted exclusively to ADD. From *Oprah* to local radio stations, ADD is being discussed. Even the wire services relate stories about children with ADD and schoolchildren selling their medication on the playground. Hardly a day passes that ADD is not discussed in some capacity.

Looking at the information being presented, one might wonder if everyone has ADD. Overdiagnosis is one of the most frequent concerns expressed by parents, educators, and mental health professionals. Ritalin bottles are flooding the offices of school nurses. In April

1995, the U.S. Department of Education issued a statement of concern that too many children are being given the "magic pill." The department has issued guidelines and two videos to help educators and parents obtain accurate diagnosis for the children suspected of having ADD.

A logical explanation for the increase in diagnosis is the heightened awareness resulting from intensive research in this area. Today, we are better informed about the disorder, and there is more reliable information and literature available. This has helped teachers and physicians recognize the symptoms of ADD earlier. More accurate and sensitive instruments are being used in the evaluation process. Because of the research being presented, federal laws are being changed to protect the rights of those with the disorder.

A question often asked is "Don't these characteristics describe everyone from time to time?" The answer is yes. However, two criteria separate ADD from the effects of everyday stress and strain: duration and intensity. ADD is not outgrown, so the characteristics are present every day for a lifetime. Second, if the symptoms interfere with the individual's ability to learn, maintain employment, socialize, and/or parent, then an evaluation for ADD may be appropriate.

To make the distinction between ADD and everyday living, it is important to understand how one acquires ADD. As mentioned previously, the characteristics of ADD are a result of how the brain is wired, not poor parenting. In many instances, professionals diagnosing for the disorder can trace back through several generations and find other family members who had similar symptoms. This has led physicians and researchers to conclude that a large number of individuals with ADD inherited the disorder. One in every four children diagnosed with ADHD has a biological parent who also has the disorder.

Head trauma or injury may result in the characteristics of ADD. Diseases that involve the brain, such as encephalitis, spinal meningitis, or AIDS, may also cause ADD symptoms to appear. Tumors in certain areas of the brain may be another cause. Peter Hauser, M.D., and his research team at the National Institute of Health, found that in rare cases a relationship could exist between generalized resistance to thyroid hormone (GRTH) and ADD. Lead poisoning, through ingestion or environmental pollution, and prenatal substance abuse (e.g., cocaine and alcohol consumption) are also listed as possible causes of attention deficit disorders.

Despite popular opinion, poor parenting and family chaos are not causes of ADD but often the result of the disorder. Food additives, sugar, and diets such as the Feingold Diet, which eliminates food additives thought to cause hyperactivity, are not scientifically proven causes of ADD. In fact, research by Mark L. Wolraich, M.D., of Vanderbilt University, has shown that diets high in sugar do not appear to affect children's learning and behavior patterns.

Some children tend to be more sensitive to certain foods and substances. Reactions to these irritants may mimic some of the characteristics of ADD. Elimination of the substances may result in improved behavior. Beyond that, maintaining a well-balanced diet is the best approach to your child's nutrition.

In summary, the disorder can be passed down through family genes or caused by disease, injury, or environmental factors. Whatever the source, it is important to remember that the changes within the brain are permanent, and ADD will not go away or be outgrown. Therefore, skills must be developed to manage the disorder for a lifetime.

All of us experience the characteristics of ADD from time to time. Periods of stress, anxiety, and depression leave us all temporarily inattentive, overactive, and/or impulsive. As we begin to stabilize and regain control of the situation, the symptoms begin to lessen.

However, with ADD, the symptoms remain no matter what is occurring in the individual's life. The longer the disorder goes undiagnosed and is mismanaged, the more intense and disabling the characteristics become. Eventually, the individual's ability to function at school, home, work, and in social situations is affected. The child struggles to keep up and succeed in school. The home is often chaotic, adding to the child's stress. Many times the parents, who may also have ADD, struggle to maintain a delicate balance.

The two criteria separating ADD from the normal ups and downs of everyday life are (1) that the symptoms are lifelong and if undiagnosed or mismanaged intensify in severity as the person ages, and (2) the disorder interferes with the individual's ability to function in at least two aspects of everyday life. This means the child may be struggling in the classroom, on the playground, at the Scout meeting, on the soccer field, in the church school class, and at home. It follows him everywhere he goes. (See *DSM IV-Criteria* in the Appendix.)

Does everyone have ADD? No, but at times we all experience the symptoms of the disorder. If you do not have ADD, during your next period of stress, when focusing and coping becomes difficult for you, take a minute to think about your child or spouse who must live with this chaos every day. Consider this time an opportunity to put yourself in touch with the ADD experience. You have "caught" ADD for just a short period, and eventually your symptoms will subside. For those diagnosed with the disorder, the symptoms will last a lifetime.

Parents who suspect their child has ADD may want to ask themselves the following questions before they call a professional for an appointment.

1. Have the symptoms I'm seeing always been there, and are they getting worse as my child gets older?
2. As an infant and toddler, did my child always seem a little different?
3. Has there been an event in my child's life that could explain a sudden change—for example, starting school, a move, entering a new school, or the moving away of a close friend? Is my child being bullied or embarrassed?
4. Has there been a major change in the family affecting my child—for example, a birth or adoption of a sibling, an illness, the death of a loved one or a pet, a separation or divorce, or the loss of a parent's job?
5. Has my child had physical and dental examinations recently? Have vision and hearing been screened?
6. If a learning disability is suspected, has the school done appropriate testing? Are services being provided?

If you have a nine-year-old daughter who suddenly is getting lost in her thoughts, there can be other influences occurring in her world that are temporarily causing ADD-like symptoms. Stress, anxiety, and depression mimic ADD and need to be considered. Therefore, a little detective work on your part can save time, money, and anxiety. If it turns out that your child has ADD, then information you gathered from your investigation will be helpful to the professional making the diagnosis.

Try to keep in mind the two criteria distinguishing ADD from symptoms mimicking the disorder. First, have you noticed the symptoms since child's infancy? Symptoms that occasionally occur and disappear once the cause is identified may mimic ADD. Second, are these symptoms seen every day in at least two parts of your child's life? If you can answer yes to both of these questions, an evaluation may be appropriate.

The diagnosis of ADD is a very complex and time-consuming process. Fifteen minutes in a doctor's office is usually not sufficient. Information must be gathered from many sources before an accurate diagnosis can be given.

How Is ADD Diagnosed?

Because ADD is a neurological disorder, meaning it involves the brain, it requires a medical diagnosis. Teachers, school psychologists and counselors, and parents are not qualified to diagnose ADD. Medical professionals experienced in recognizing and evaluating ADD need to make the diagnosis. These professionals include psychiatrists (a medical doctor), clinical psychologists, and neurologists. Often pediatricians can be included in this list, but many are now referring to the professionals listed above as being more experienced in this area.

The school plays a vital role in the diagnosis of ADD. While they should not be making the diagnosis, teachers and other school personnel are usually the first to suspect that a child has ADD. If other learning problems are suspected, the school psychologist may evaluate for learning disabilities or other learning issues. The speech and language pathologist may evaluate for language processing concerns (how well the child uses and understands language both in print and orally). The school counselor may investigate for possible emotional concerns. A social worker may look at family issues, and an occupational therapist may examine the child's sensory integration capabilities. Teachers complete checklists and relate their classroom observations. All of the information collected by the school is an essential part of the child's evaluation.

While the school is gathering information, a physical, and perhaps dental, examination of the child may be requested. Vision and hearing may also be tested.

As all of these other professionals are evaluating the child in their areas of expertise, the ADD expert is also collecting information. There is no specific test for ADD. Parents will be interviewed by the evaluator. They also may be asked to supply family histories to see if other family members have demonstrated similar symptoms. Prenatal and developmental histories of the child will be requested. A typical day at home and school will be shared. Both parents and teachers will be asked to fill out checklists and questionnaires.

The child also will be interviewed by the evaluator. Pencil-and-paper tests and computer testing may be included. The professional will evaluate for any of the related disorders mentioned in the previous section "The Who, What, and Why."

The evaluator is putting all the pieces of the puzzle together to get a complete picture of the child. The pieces not fitting will be eliminated and the remaining parts will result in a diagnosis.

As you can see, an accurate diagnosis is a long process involving many professionals working together to examine every possible reason for your child's actions. Other conditions imitating ADD are depression, emotional upsets, anxiety, stress, mood disorders, learning disabilities, and language processing disabilities. It takes an expert to sort out all of the factors involved.

Fifteen minutes in a doctor's office without input from anyone else may result in an inaccurate diagnosis. Almost any child can sit still and stay focused in a new environment for fifteen minutes. The whole picture is not seen if a diagnosis is based on this limited, uninformed experience.

In summary, an evaluation of your child should include the following:

1. An experienced, qualified medical professional who coordinates the collection of information.
2. Family, medical, and developmental histories supplied by parents, as well as information about the daily functioning of the family and child.
3. Schools do not diagnose for ADD but are a very important part of the diagnosis. They can supply information about learning and/or language disabilities, classroom observations, social interaction, and emotional concerns.
4. Physical and dental checkups, as well as vision and hearing screening, if requested to eliminate any physical causes.
5. Checklists and questionnaires completed by parents and teachers, if asked by the evaluator.
6. The ruling out of conditions mimicking ADD.
7. Identification of any comorbid, or related diorders such as ODD, LD, etc.

By now you probably have an understanding of the complexity of this disorder. That is why having an experienced professional who will look at all the explanations of what could be affecting your child is so very important. Finding this professional could be difficult. Check with local ADD support groups for a list of resources in your area. Below are some questions to guide you in the selection of a potential evaluator.

1. What percentage of the evalualtor's patients have been diagnosed ADD? (Twenty to 30 percent would be average.)
2. How does he or she make the diagnosis? What tests, checklists, information, and other professionals does he or she include in the process?

3. Does he or she contact and work with the school? This is very important. The school offers vital information and needs to be supported after a diagnosis is made.
4. If the child is diagnosed with ADD, how does he or she manage the disorder? A collaborative approach, not just a Ritalin pill, is the appropriate answer.

The complexity of making a thorough diagnosis may be very overwhelming. To sort it out, the process described in this chapter should be followed. Because there is no single test for ADD, even this process is not perfect. However, by involving everyone who works closely with your child, you will diminish the chances for error. Once a diagnosis is made, pull together the team of experts to offer support to you and your child as you begin your journey down the highway of managing the ADD.

A Partnership of Professionals

An African proverb states, "It takes a village to raise a child." To support a child with ADD, this is especially true. Managing ADD and finding ways to help your child build lifelong skills can be an overwhelming and tiring job. Uniting a team of experts to support you and your child is an important step.

The physician making the diagnosis may recommend medication therapy. This is a very frightening step for parents. Understandably, parents are very resistant to giving their child medication. Asking questions and requesting reading material about the medication is an important part of the decision-making process.

Asking a doctor you can trust to discuss with you the following ten questions may give you the information you are seeking.

1. How does the recommended medication work? Depending on the nature of the diagnosis, some physicians use stimulants such as Ritalin or Dexedrine, and others may prescribe antidepressants, such as Desipramine.

2. What symptoms will this medication affect? What differences will be noticed? These might include increased attention or reduced activity levels.

3. What won't be affected by the prescribed medication? For example, learning disabilities or poor social skills may not be eliminated.

4. What is your family history? Has alcoholism or depression been noted? How about Tourette syndrome (a disorder that involves involuntary movements, or tics)? If there is a family history of Tourette, stimulants may not be recommended.

5. Which symptoms are the most problematic? By prioritizing, the physician can select the medication to ease the symptom most interfering with the child's ability to function.

6. What are the expectations? There is no magic pill. Medication is just part of the whole management effort. Ideally, the level of medication given should be such that the symptoms are eased enough to allow the child to begin skill development.

7. What changes have taken place? When evaluating the effectiveness of the medication, consider all the factors involved. Misbehavior or increased distractibility may be due to anxiety, poor self-esteem, peer problems, or increased frustration, rather than ADD.

8. What other strategies are you using? Medication is never the complete answer. Bypass strategies may be needed in the classroom and at home. Therapy and counseling may also be a part of the whole management plan.

9. What should you avoid? Asking, "Did you take your medicine today?" gives the impression that the medication is responsible for the child's behavior.

10. What are the possible side effects? Communicate with the physician and carefully monitor your child's medication. Ask how the medication may affect your child and what changes should be reported back to the doctor.

One last thought about medication. Edward Hallowell, M.D., author of a book about ADD called *Driven to Distraction,* raises an interesting point. Often taking medication for ADD is compared with taking insulin to control diabetes. Dr. Hallowell points out that without insulin, the diabetic could die, but medication for ADD is not necessary for survival. Therefore, taking medication for ADD is like wearing eyeglasses. Glasses help correct and focus vision. The medications prescribed for ADD help the mind to focus. Wearing glasses and taking medication for ADD are choices made to improve the quality of life. They are not necessary to maintain life.

Once a decision has been made to medicate your child, it is the physician's responsibility to select the appropriate medication to ease the symptoms identified. Unless Tourette syndrome is in the child's medical history, Ritalin, a stimulant, is usually the drug of choice. Because of manufacturing inconsistencies, it is recommended that the brand name Ritalin, not the generic drug methylphenidate hydrochloride, be prescribed if your insurance allows. Dexedrine and Cylert are the other stimulant medications often used. Depending on the diagnosis and involvement of other disorders, medications such as Imipramine, Desipramine, or Prozac may be prescribed. (See "Medications Commonly Prescribed to Improve Behavior, Mood, and Learning" in Appendix G.)

When several severe symptoms are present, many physicians begin with one medication to alleviate the primary symptom and gradually add a second medication to ease the other symptoms.

Whenever medication is being used, it is your physician's responsibility to frequently and consistently monitor its effects. Neither the parents nor the school should accept this responsibility. The teachers and the parents need to keep the doctor informed of changes or side effects they observe or that the child relates to them.

Since neither author has a medical background, we refer you to your physician or pharmacist for more information.

Along with the medication therapy, individual and/or family therapy may be a part of your support system. Learning more about ADD and how it is affecting your child and the family is very important. Often the family is in chaos, and parents benefit from learning how to cope with the stress. Learning how to effectively maintain consistency in the home is an important part of the management system. Siblings are often angry and embarrassed by the child with ADD, who seems to get all the attention. They feel left out or ignored. These issues need to be addressed. How to cope with relatives and neighbors is another matter to be discussed. A psychiatrist, psychologist, social worker, or counselor can be your mental health partner.

At school, teachers learning how to modify the classroom are an important part of your support team. Many of the suggestions in this book can be modified for use in the classroom. They require no money and little time commitment. If teachers keep in mind their objectives for a lesson, they can modify their teaching to meet the needs of all students.

Tutors, resource teachers, speech and language pathologists, occupational therapists, school nurses, counselors, and/or school psychologists should be a part of your school support team. They can supply special services to your child and offer additional support to the classroom teacher. Not all schools have all these service personnel available. However, utilize the services your school does provide.

As a quick review, your ADD support system should include as many of the following professionals as are required to meet the specific needs of your child.

1. A psychiatrist, clinical psychologist, neurologist, or pediatrician to test and diagnose.
2. A pediatrician or psychiatrist to administrate and monitor medications. Your pharmacist can also be a source of information.
3. A psychiatrist, psychologist, social worker, or counselor, to provide family and individual therapy.
4. Educators, tutors, resource teachers, a speech and language pathologist, a school nurses, a school counselor and/or psychologist, and the school principal to offer support throughout the school day.
5. An occupational therapist specializing in sensory integration to provide therapy in body management.

The management of ADD is a multimodal, or team, approach. It is too large and overwhelming a job to be accomplished by just the parents. Everyone working together, supporting each other, is the most effective and constructive way to support the child.

With the increasing amount of research and information available, changes have been occurring in state and federal laws. Parents and members of their support team should become knowledgeable about these laws and how the child's rights are being protected. Advocating to get the "reasonable" accommodations that will help your child succeed is a very important part of the management process.

Protecting Your Child's Rights

Understanding how the law protects the rights of children with ADD is very important. In September 1991, the U.S. Department of Education issued a "Policy Clarification Memorandum" (see Appendix H). This publication recognized that children with ADD were eligible for special education and related services based solely on their diagnosis of ADD if the disability interfered with their ability to learn.

Children with disabilities qualify for assistance under two existing federal laws. Public Law 94-142, Part B, pertains to the Individuals with Disabilities Act (IDEA) and is enforced by the Office of Special Education and Rehabilitative Services in the Department of Education. Section 504 of the Rehabilitation Act of 1973 is enforced by the Office of Civil Rights. Both are in place to ensure a free and appropriate public education for all children. Under the Americans with Disabilities Act (ADA) federal guidelines are set for private schools without religious affiliation. Private institutions receiving federal funding may not discriminate against children with disabilities.

Under IDEA, school districts are required to write an Individual Education Plan (IEP) for children who are identified with one or more of the twelve qualifying disabilities. The evaluation process may be requested by the school or the parents and must take place within a reasonable period of time once the parents sign the "Permission to

Test" form. Parents should be an equal partner with the school in the writing of the child's IEP. An IEP must include the following:

1. A description of the disability and the present level of performance.
2. Annual goals and short-term objectives.
3. Specific educational services to be provided for the child.
4. Regularly scheduled evaluation procedures to determine progress.
5. Dates services begin and end.
6. Extent of participation in regular education programs.

Section 504 defines a qualifying handicap. It provides for services solely on the basis of ADD *if* the disorder infers with learning, which is a major life function. Some children will qualify for services under both IDEA and Section 504; others may qualify only under 504.

The federal law sets the minimum standards to be met. Each state department of education defines the law and sets the requirements for the school districts within the state. Ask your state department of education for information on Section 504 and your child's rights.

Many states are requiring school districts to have 504 coordinators who are required to write 504 plans for children diagnosed with ADD. It is similar to an Individualized Education Plan (IEP) written for children under IDEA. The 504 plan lists the specific modifications that will be made in the general education classroom and the strategies and interventions that will be implemented to help the child with ADD succeed.

Research is causing changes in the way lawmakers view ADD. When ADD interferes with a person's ability to function, protection is now available under federal law. IEPs and 504 plans emphasize the strengths of the child and attempt to bypass or remediate weaknesses. It is through the child's strengths that he will succeed in the school experience and decide the career path he will follow into adulthood.

Because ADD is not outgrown, recent federal legislation is also designed to protect the rights of the adult with ADD, making his journey through life more promising.

Is There a Child Under all Those Labels?

As the child progresses into adulthood, he may pick up labels describing his differences. Sometimes it seems we lose the child under all the labels. There is ADD, ADHD, LD, SI, TS, ODC, ODD, and CD, just to list a few. If we are not careful, the labels become the child's identity.

Because of the increasing number of labels in society today, there is a growing resistance to having children evaluated. There are several reasons why an evaluation by an experienced professional is important.

From a personal perspective, when Nancy's son Christian was diagnosed with ADD, several things happened. First, the burden of guilt and poor parenting was lifted off Christian's parents' shoulders. There was a medical explanation for his behavior. It was beyond their control. As parents, they had coped and managed as best they could with the information they had.

Second, Nancy's husband, David, was diagnosed with ADD at the same time. It finally made sense why the things Christian did never bothered him, and why he would always assure Nancy that Christian would turn out all right. After all, he had survived his "adventuresome" childhood and adolescence. Already successful in his career, David knew he was capable and intelligent. However, until college, he never did well in school. This diagnosis provided the explanation that put his past to rest.

Perhaps the most important reason for getting the evaluation was to hear Christian respond, "You mean I'm not stupid? There is another reason why, no matter how hard I try, I never seem to do anything right?" What a sense of relief to know it was something beyond his control. How comforting to know it was not a lack of intelligence. In fact, he discovered he was very intelligent. What a burden taken off his shoulders.

As an educator, Nancy recognizes that teachers need to be informed about how the child will demonstrate the ADD. Because of the complexity of the disorder and the uniqueness of the brain, each child will manifest the disorder differently. Knowing how the ADD affects the child will help teachers better understand the child's performance and how to meet the individual child's needs. Working from the team approach, Nancy found it helpful to have the professional who made Christian's diagnosis visit his school and explain to his teachers how his ADD specifically is demonstrated. That professional became a resource for Christian's teachers.

As a learning specialist, Nancy uses the same collaboration technique. The psychiatrists and psychologists of the students with ADD are a support and resource not only to the parents and children but also to Nancy and the teaching staff. Together they focus on the strengths of the child and develop a management plan of action.

After the diagnosis, it is important to shift the focus from the label to the child. The label is a way of identifying the problem. Once the problem has been identified, the focus needs to be placed back on the child. In focusing on the child, the solutions can be found.

Strength Identification

Identifying the strengths and weaknesses of the child is the place to begin. Everyone, especially the child, can easily list the weaknesses. Listing strengths may take more effort. However, the earlier the strengths are identified and supported, the better. Figure 2-1 lists numerous strengths your child may possess. Think about your child's many talents, and with your child make a list of the strengths unique to him or her.

Building on the strengths you identify in Figure 2-1 is the key to the success of your child. Both parents and teachers need to be aware of and utilize the strengths to help the child experience success.

At school, opportunities should be given to tap the resources of all children in the classroom. For example, a book report is assigned and the child must give a report to show he read and understood the book. Unless the objective of this assignment is to work on writing skills, each child should be able to complete the assignment in his

Figure 2-1
Idea Creators—Possible Strengths

Strengths to Build On
Good at math
Reads well
Very artistic
Expresses self well
Sings well
Good gross motor skills (athletic)
Good social skills
Patient
Good computer skills
Creative
Artistic
Good auditory memory
Good visual memory
Strong abstract reasoning
Neat handwriting
Makes friends easily
Good problem solver
Neat
Very organized
Hard worker
Good phonetic skills
Kind to younger children
Kind to elders
Carpentry skills
Likes to fish
Can cast a baitcaster
Ecologically minded
Loves outdoors
Likes gardening
Can cut grass
Good with animals
Plays an instrument
Can sing
Has mechanical skills
Volunteers at church or school
Can cook
Can read and follow a recipe
Takes care of pet
Can run the washer
Can build model rockets
Can fly a kite
Is interested in history (Civil War or WWII)
Likes to travel
Interested in space

area of strength. The artistic child might design a book cover. The athletic child could do a dance. The musically talented child could write a song or rap. Each child, creating in his area of strength, can find success.

As your child progresses through school, guiding him in his areas of strengths becomes more important. By high school, closely examining career choices takes a priority. If the child's strengths have been identified, selecting a career that will utilize those strengths will offer a successful future. Christian, having strong oral and written language skills, is pursuing a degree in communications. Being weak in math and science, he ruled out medicine or finance as career choices.

Be cautious about placing your child in a specific learning or occupational track because you've been told he doesn't have the skills to be competent. Many children who have struggled in elementary school begin to flourish as the curriculum changes in high school or college where their strengths can be accentuated.

This is a time for parents to be realistic. No matter how much your child wants to be an artist, if he cannot draw and has no sense of color, this may not be an appropriate choice. However, if he has good verbal and organizational skills, he might consider combining his strengths and his love for art by working in an art gallery or museum promoting and displaying works of art.

Take a few minutes and complete the strengths sheet (Figure 2-2). Include your child in this exercise. It is important for him or her to identify individual strengths. Keep this strengths sheet handy, and pull it out when you begin to lose focus. Share it with your child often when discouragement or frustration appear. Share it with your child's teachers and ask them to begin using the strengths identified. This can serve as a tool to keep the focus on your child's talents and shift from the negative to the positive. Once you know and understand your child's strengths, you are ready to build a management plan that utilizes them.

Figure 2–2
My List of Strengths

_____

_____

_____

_____

_____

_____

_____

_____

_____

_____

_____

_____

_____

_____

_____

_____

_____

_____

_____

_____

_____

_____

3

Symptoms Management

Since 1980 there have been three hallmark characteristics associated with attention deficit disorders. They are inattention, hyperactivity, and impulsivity. In this section we will examine each characteristic separately. A symptoms checklist and management ideas that parents may want to consider using will be provided at the end of each section. (See Appendix A for *DSM IV* criteria for AD/HD.) This also would be the time to also have your child's strength sheet available. Once the symptoms have been identified, focus on your child's srtengths to select the strategies that may be most successful. With this in mind, let's begin by examining the intricacies of inattention.

Heads on a Swivel and Mind Journeys

Inattention is one of the three hallmark characteristics of attention deficit disorders. An individual with only the inattention component is diagnosed with attention deficit/hyperactivity disorder, predominantly inattentive type. Those who are inattentive as well as hyperactive and impulsive are diagnosed AD/HD, predominatly hyperactive/impulsive type. Those with all three sympotms are diagnosed AD/HD, combined type.

Inattention, or distractibility, is defined as being drawn or diverted away from something claiming attention. A common misconception is that individuals with ADD cannot pay attention. This is not true. The problem is they pay attention to everything.

This is thought to occur because the brain's filtering system, or reticular formation, is not functioning properly. The reticular formation filters distractions the way a drip coffeemaker filters coffee. If you put the coffee in the filter and the water in the tank, you can get a pot of coffee. However, if you fill the tank and forget to put in the filter basket, water goes everywhere and what does go into the pot is not coffee. Of course this example is an oversimplification of the brain's filtering process. However, it may give you a mental picture of why the brain's inability to filter distractions results in the inattention. This is another example of ADD as the invisible disorder.

When a child's brain has problems filtering, you might, for example, see him watch a pencil roll off a desk, which causes him to see the fish swimming in the tank just as someone passes by the window. While looking out the window, he hears a siren wailing three blocks away. This is the child with his "head on a swivel." The child, distracted by his surroundings, hears and sees everything. Everything, that is, but the teacher who just explained how to add decimals. Therefore, ADD is not the inability to attend but the inability to selectively attend and to filter out all the distractions. Listening to the teacher's explanation is an example of selective attention.

Another form of inattention is the child who is inwardly distracted. These children go on wonderful "mind journeys." The teacher reads the spelling word *farm*. Rather than thinking about how to spell the word *farm*, the child with ADD begins to think about the farm her grandparents own. She thinks about all the animals and the great adventures she had on her last visit. She thinks about her grandparents and is reminded of their last visit at Christmas. This then reminds her of the bike she received, and she thinks maybe she will go for a bike ride after school with her friend. If the teacher has not noticed by this time that this child has tuned out and is three spelling words behind, the mind journeys continue until something jars the child back to the present.

The inward inattention is more subtle than the child who is constantly looking around. Females frequently fall into the mind-journey category. These are children who sit quietly in class, do not disturb anyone, but have a faraway look in their eyes.

Inattention can interfere with functioning in any situation. The scenario can sound like a Charlie Brown cartoon when the adults speak. However, this situation has little humor. The child is only hearing bits and pieces of the conversation. A sample of what an inattentive child might be hearing may go like this: "Class, it is time to take blah, blah, blah book and open to page blah. Blah, blah, blah to study about blah. Blah, blah, blah, blah, blah. And now for homework. . . ."

Homework? What is going on? The child is scrambling again to find out the information she missed and causing others to lose patience with her. She has missed out on another learning opportunity. Once again, she has to ask, "What am I supposed to do?" after a ten-minute explanation has just been given. She is frustrated, the teacher is frustrated, and so are her classmates.

At home, you ask your child to clean his room. A half hour later you discover one of two things. Either he never made it to his room and is watching television, or he is in his room, amid all the chaos, reading a book he uncovered when he began to clean.

Does this mean he is defying you? Not necessarily. This may be your child's ADD in action. Between leaving you and his bedroom, he got distracted by the television and forgot your request. Or if he made it to his room, he became so overwhelmed by the chaos, he did not know where to begin, so he easily got distracted by a book he picked up.

This particular behavior would drive Nancy crazy. She would

send Christian to his "black hole" to find the carpet. An hour later when she checked on his progress, he was happily reading or playing with a long-lost toy. Nothing had been done. She rolled up her sleeves and began the process of cleaning while muttering about his poor wife. What she discovered was that if she gave Christian a specific area to clean, he was able to complete it with minimal distraction.

Becoming older and wiser in the process of living and rearing a child easily sidetracked (he was not diagnosed at this time), Nancy tried some experiments. Instead of telling Christian to go clean his room, she wrote a list of what needed to be done.

1. Pick up dirty clothes and put in hamper.
2. Pick up clean clothes and put in drawers.
3. Put books on shelves.

Christian could begin with any task he wanted but had to cross off each job as it was completed.

This idea was helpful, but it still seemed to take him forever to get the job finished. Therefore, she began to set time limits. She had him set his watch alarm for what she considered a reasonable time to do the job. When the alarm went off, she checked his progress. This worked fairly well. However, by accident, she discovered that nothing worked better than scheduling a room cleaning before he planned to go out to play, or go to the movies, or ride his bike.

Nancy asked for a thorough cleaning about once a month and realized that her and Christian's definitions were not the same. She also came to realize that Christian's chaos *was* his organizational system, and she respected that by not interfering in the cleaning process.

It is important to realize there is a fine line between defiance and disorder. Parenting children with ADD can be a tiring and stressful experience. Therefore, it is best to step back, look closely at the situation, and to determine if your child is trying to drive you crazy or if you are seeing the ADD. Examples given above are clearly those of inattentive children. The children would have complied if something had not distracted them. Remember that children want to please.

However, children with ADD do not always have the skills needed to do what is asked. Through trial and error and *practice,* the skills can be learned.

To help you recognize the ways in which your child demonstrates his or her inattention, we have provided an inattention-symptoms checklist (Figure 3-1). Take a few minutes to sit down with your child and identify all the symptoms that apply to him or her. Add other characteristics not included. Keep this checklist handy and refer to it whenever you become confused or overwhelmed. Share the symptoms with your child's teachers and support staff to help them better understand how ADD affects your child.

A Chinese proverb states, "If you give a man a fish, he will eat for a day. If you teach a man to fish, he will eat for a lifetime." Because ADD is not outgrown, the goal is to teach your child the skills he or she will use for a lifetime. This will not happen overnight. However, with consistency and persistence, progress will occur. The small changes that you begin to notice day after day will be your indication that a new skill is being mastered.

Once you have determined if and how your child demonstrates the inattention component of ADD, you may want to try some of the strategies listed below. This is by no means a complete list. It is a starting place from which you can create and add your own interventions to meet your child's needs. To avoid becoming overwhelmed, try only one or two at a time. As your child begins to develop and use the new skills, gradually add others.

You may want to keep a record of the strategies that are successfully helping your child manage his ADD. Share those interventions with your child's teacher, because any of the ideas offered can be easily adapted for use in the classroom.

1. Make sure you have eye contact by calling the child's name. Verbal cues such as a nonsense word or "I need to see your eyes" may help. Also, have the child look at the person to whom he is speaking.
2. Secret signals, such as pointing to the nose, a wink, or a tug on

Figure 3–1
Symptoms of Inattention

HOME

Easily distracted by what is going on around him.

Often appears to be lost in own thoughts and a million miles away.

Sometimes overfocuses, especially when involved in new or exciting activity such as Nintendo, Legos, TV.

Needs to have things repeated over and over.

Difficulty following routines without supervision.

Slow to action. Takes forever getting dressed, eating breakfast, getting ready to leave.

Bedroom a disaster area.

Homework time is battle of wills. Needs supervision to complete assignments.

Constantly losing glasses, jackets, supplies, or toys.

SCHOOL

Missing assignments.

Loses things often.

Comes to class unprepared. Books, supplies, notes missing.

Has poor organizational skills. (Seen in locker, desk, note taking, materials to go home.)

Inconsistant performance, grades range from 95 to 59.

Poor test performance.

Difficulty taking notes, copying from board or overhead.

Stares into space often.

Asks what to do after clear explanation given.

Difficulty working independently.

SOCIAL

Makes inappropriate or delayed responses.

Appears tuned out or bored.

Has difficulty making and keeping friends.

Doesn't follow rules.

Doesn't understand social cues. Can't read facial expressions.

Attention is caught by other environmental stimuli.

Doesn't appear to be listening to friends.

Starts and stops activities.

Can't find toys.

Forgetful. May forget promises to friends.

the ear, may cue the child. Standing near the child or putting a hand on his shoulder can bring back attention. Directing attention to where the child should be focusing also helps.

3. Children with ADD often get overwhelmed by receiving too much information at one time. These are the children who sit and do nothing. They literally need a starting place. When Tim was in the fifth grade, his teacher sent him to the library with a five-page list of acceptable books for the upcoming book report. She was at a loss to understand why, with all those choices, he couldn't select a book. The task needs to appear manageable. Listed are some strategies to accomplish this.
   - Fold back the book so only one page is visible.
   - Use bookmarks or the three middle fingers to mark one line at a time.
   - Use cover sheets or "windows" to see only one question at a time. Many children get so overwhelmed by the twenty-fifth problem, they cannot begin the first.

4. If you say it, write it. The written reminder lasts when the child gets distracted along the way. Try the following to build additional skills.
   - Give clear, simple directions, no more than two at a time.
   - Ask the child to repeat back the direction to check for attention and understanding.
   - Give written versions of all directions.
   - Use lists. Have the child cross off each task as completed. This not only provides a sense of accomplishment but serves as a map for the child to follow.
   - Chart morning and evening routines and have the child check off each as completed.
   - In his video *Why Won't My Child Pay Attention,* Dr. Sam Goldstein, Ph.D., suggests having your child become a deejay and make a tape recording of the routines. Parents start the prerecorded tape in the morning. As the first song ends, your child's recorded message reminds him he should be out of bed. As song two begins, he may announce during the

next two songs he will get dressed. The process continues until the morning routine is completed. Hearing his or her own voice give the commands can be effective and take the burden of nagging off the parents. It's fun, too.

- Have a large calendar available to chart chores and other important reminders. You might use a different color for each family member.
- Have the child write out a schedule each evening of what needs to be completed for homework.
- Alternate a pencil-and-paper task at a table with a more informal task, such as reading or studying, at another location. Again, each task should be crossed off as completed.
- Have only the materials at the workplace needed to complete the task. Put all materials away before beginning the next task.

5. Experiment with music. For some children with ADD, a totally silent room can be very distracting. Either background music without words or white noise can be very effective. Household noises such as the hum of the dishwasher or refrigerator can accomplish the same purpose as music. Other children must have total quiet in order to concentrate.

6. Timers can be effective. Working within the time limit can keep the child focused. Judgment should be used as to when timers would be helpful. They can be very useful to time a break or a time-out, while doing chores, when preparing to leave, or when following a routine. For example, "The bus is coming in ten minutes; I'm setting the timer" can be an effective way to prepare for leaving the house on time. Or "You have twenty minutes to clean your room; I'm setting the timer" may get the job finished more efficiently.

   Timing schoolwork or other tasks where accuracy is expected would not be appropriate. However, having your child estimate how long a task may take to finish can be effective in getting a job done.

7. Children who procrastinate or are difficult to get moving in the

morning may benefit from laying out their clothes the night before. This eliminates the morning hassle of having to make decisions about what to wear and eliminates power struggles over clothing choices. Preparing lunches and having the schoolbag by the door the night before can result in a calmer start to the day.

8. Make several study carrels from cardboard and contact paper for you child's teacher to have available in the classroom for any of the children to use when they want the privacy of an "office."

9. Supply your child with earplugs to muffle classroom and household noises.

10. In the classroom, especially when children are taking tests, allowing the child with ADD additional time can be a great gift. Three options might be considered. One would be to allow the child to test with the rest of the class and complete the test at a later time. The second option would be to allow the child to test out of class, where distractions are limited and time is not a factor. A third option would be to allow the child to take the test and then orally retest the questions missed to improve the grade. Approach your child's teacher about modifying the testing situations.

Body in Motion

The second hallmark characteristic is hyperactivity. If inattention is not noted, children with hyperactivity receive the diagnosis attention deficit/hyperactivity disorders, predominantly hyperactive/impulsive type. These children are often inattentive as well as hyperactive (combined type), but the inability to regulate the body's need to move is the more interfering symptom. Hyperactivity is the only characteristic that diminishes as the child ages. By adolescence, hyperactivity lessens as impulsivity increases. However, many adults who were hyperactive as children maintain high levels of activity.

Hyperactivity is a state of constant motion. A trip to the pool in the summer is bound to bring a loud "Walk!" from the lifeguard. Ask him to scamper, skip, hop, scoot, and snake across the walkway, aisle, or room and you might be more easily accommodated. But walk? It would be easier if he were asked to stand on his head. We run down, but this child's motor never stops. He just keeps going and going and going.

Children who are hyperactive are constantly fidgeting and manipulating objects. Chewing on pencils, pens, erasers, buttons, and anything handy is also common. Teachers used to ask Nancy if she fed Christian, because he would chew off his buttons and then began "feasting" on his shirt collar.

Children with AD/HD find it difficult to remain seated in the classroom or at the dinner table or workplace. They are much more comfortable standing, rocking, or sitting in some contorted position. This movement is often the way information is processed.

Not only are their bodies in motion but also their minds are racing. As one thought enters their head, it is pushed out of the way by four or five more right behind it.

Many children with hyperactivity function on only a few hours of sleep, awaking refreshed and ready to go. Exhausted parents get little relief. They dare not leave the child unsupervised for safety reasons. Climbing to great heights and constantly running about put children with AD/HD at greater risk for falls and accidents.

Parents also receive a lot of criticism because it appears they are unable to control their child. Relatives and friends are more than willing to make suggestions and recommendations on how to discipline the child. This only makes the parents feel more stressed and inadequate.

The important thing to keep in mind is that your child's high activity level is beyond his control. His body and mind are stuck in high gear. It is not a result of poor parenting!

Bear in mind that the child with AD/HD learns through motion. To ask these children to sit and be quiet is an unreasonable request that sets them up for failure. Often the following scenario occurs. The child wants to please the adult. He knows his constant movement is very disturbing. Therefore, he decides he will try to keep his body quiet. So much concentration goes into containing his energy that he is not aware of anything else going on around him. At home, parents may think they are being ignored when he fails to respond to them. In the classroom, he may miss an entire lesson trying not to draw attention to himself.

Within the child's mind, the following struggle may be occurring: "I won't get Miss Smith angry today. I'll keep my hands still. No, I won't roll my pencil around on my desktop. Good, my hands are quiet. Oh, no! There goes my foot. I've got to stop that tapping. I'm wiggling! How much longer to recess? I can't sit here much longer!" During this mental battle, the boy missed out on the teacher's explanation. But he was sitting quietly!

To manage this hyperactivity, a compromise needs to be established. The compromise is that as adults, we recognize the child's need to move is beyond his or her control. Then we need to set boundaries to define where that movement would be appropriate and acceptable. Take, for example, the child who drums on the table during mealtime. The compromise would be the parents' recognition of the child's need to release energy by allowing him to drum on his leg or the cushion of the chair rather than the tabletop.

In the classroom, the child who is constantly fidgeting in his desk needs to channel energy elsewhere. Therefore, the teacher needs to recognize the child's need to fidget and give her something to manipulate. A small ball she can discreetly hold in her hand would be an excellent compromise.

Figure 3-2 has been provided to identify how your child demonstrates this characteristic. Complete the checklist with your child and add other symptoms your child displays. Refer to this checklist often to help keep the disability in perspective. Remember to share it with your child's teachers and support personnel.

After you have completed the checklist, you may want to examine

Figure 3–2
Symptoms of Hyperactivity

HOME

Never sits still. Always on the go.
Fidgets constantly.
Requires little sleep or has difficulty falling asleep.
Picks up objects and manipulates them.
Wanders off in public.
Talks excessively.
Spills or knocks over objects often.
Uncomfortable in confined places.

SCHOOL

Out of seat often.
Uncomfortable sitting. Stands, rocks, raps, swivels, twirls or contorts—
especially when completing a task.
Fidgets at desk.
Chews on objects—pencils, pens, erasers, clothing.
Difficulty standing in line.
Skips, hops, runs but seldom walks.

SOCIAL

Constant, unexpected energy that often makes peers apprehensive.
Always touching others or their belongings.
Restlessness.
May absentmindedly throw sticks or rocks.

management strategies listed below. Select one or two at a time; implementation of too many at once can be overwhelming. Your goal is to find the combination best fitting the symptoms identified in the checklist and use the strategies to develop new skills that will last a lifetime. Don't forget your child's strengths sheet. Select strategies that will reinforce and utilize his strengths.

Once you find the strategies that are building management skills, record them and share them with your child's teachers. The following strategies can be easily used in the classroom.

1. Recognize the need for the child's body to move.
2. Find an acceptable way to allow that motion to take place.
3. Use a secret signal to cue the child to raise his hand or wait his turn. Sometimes a finger to the lips or modeling the motion (raising your hand) is helpful.
4. Allow the child to manipulate an object to channel his energy.
5. Remove the shoes of toe tappers.
6. Give your child space in which to move. Rope or tape off an area that can be your child's own space. In a confined facility such as a church or theater, sit in the back and leave an empty chair next to the child or seat him on the end of the row.
7. Anticipate the situation ahead of time and find ways to prepare the child. For example, if eating out with your child is a disaster, plan ahead. Explain before leaving the house that you are going to McDonald's for dinner. Set down the rules, e.g., "If there is any running around, we will leave immediately." (Be sure you state only what you are willing to do.) Give your child a job at the restaurant to allow for movement, such as ordering the meal, paying for it, carrying a tray, getting the napkins, or cleaning up.
8. Allow children to stand rather than sit if this is a more comfortable position.
9. Allow for frequent breaks after short work sessions. When making a homework schedule, include a break after each task. This not only refreshes the child but is also an incentive to complete the task. (Set a timer to get the child back to work.)
10. Allow your child time to unwind after school. Homework should not occur until your child has had a chance to relax.
11. Keep your child involved in activities that allow for the release of energy. Organized or individual sports such as swimming, biking, Rollerblading, gymnastics, dancing, or Tae Kwon Do are good choices.
12. Have a time-out or quiet place where your child can go and calm down when he loses control or becomes overstimulated.

Acting Without Thinking

The third hallmark characteristic of ADD is impulsivity. Impulsive children may also be hyperactive and/or inattentive. While hyperactivity tends to diminish in adolesence, impulsivity intensifies.

Impulsivity is acting without giving thought to the consequences of those actions. Impulsive children lack the ability to monitor their actions and verbal responses. They usually jump in feet first without being aware of where they will land.

The impulsive child is the one who leaves a church service and ends up in the emergency room. What else would you do with a quarter in your hand but pop it in your mouth? Of course, when it hits the "hangy-down thing," you have no choice but to swallow it! Who said parenting a child with ADD was dull? They take us to places where no other parent dares to tread.

Impulsivity is not a lack of "moral control." It does not mean the parents have not taught the children manners or the difference between right and wrong. Impulsive children do not take the time to stop and think, "If I do this, this will occur. Is this what I want to happen?"

Often they alienate their peers. Waiting for their turn seems an impossible task. They make insulting or offensive comments, hurting the feelings of other people. Reading social cues is very difficult. Afraid they will forget their ideas, they constantly blurt out answers and interrupt conversations. Thinking they know what to do, they will begin a task before they have all the instructions. Impulsive children lack organizational skills and often jump from one activity to another without completing anything. The constant desire to buy and spend is the insatiable side of this symptom.

The impulsive child is constantly apologizing. He is truly surprised and sorry when he realizes he has hurt someone's feelings, yet he will turn right around and make the same mistake again. This child may be unaware he is the cause of the chaos and often very remorseful for things he has done. This is one difference between the child with ADD and one with an aggressive personality.

Impulsivity is probably the most difficult of the hallmark characteristics to bring under control. As the child ages, hyperactivity tends to decrease, but impulsivity increases in the teen years. Therefore, developing management skills early is very important.

Awareness is the key to managing impulsivity. The child needs to learn to stop and think before acting. Usually, if he can stop long enough to consider the results of his actions, he will make appropriate choices. Helping the child to look before he leaps can prevent significant heartache.

Sometimes a visual reminder can be very effective. Any symbol you and your child agree on can work. To help Christian control his impulsivity, Nancy used stars as the visual cue. Stars are simple, positive symbols that reminded him to stop and think before he acted. For Christian, STAR was an acronym for Stop, Think, Act Responsibly. We bombarded him with stars. They were all over the house, in the car, in his plan book, on his lunch, and in his locker. The teachers put a star on the blackboard and made eye contact with him when they noticed him losing control. This proved to be an effective way to help him develop awareness about his actions.

Teachers especially like the STAR concept and use it with much success. STAR can have several different meanings. It can mean Stop, Think, Act Responsibly to the child who loses control. For the child who races through his work, it can mean Stop, Think, and Review. Stop, Think, and Respond might help the child who makes inappropriate comments or interrupts. The star cues the child to check his behavior.

A teacher in one classroom placed a paper star on the upper corner of each desk. She explained to her students that the star was there to help them monitor their actions. Whenever a child needed a reminder, she would walk by, point to the star, and keep going. The learner instantly got the silent message and responded appropriately.

Once we can help our children stop long enough to think, they need to learn to mentally ask "if-then" questions. "If I say this, then what will result?" or "If I do that, then what will happen?" If the child can determine the results ahead of time, then he can adjust his actions before they occur. This sounds easy but is extremely difficult and takes consistent repetition of this technique over a long period.

Sometimes preparing the child ahead of time can be helpful. Talk to your child about what expectations you have of him. For example, if when you take your child grocery shopping he is in the habit of throwing a tantrum and demanding you buy him everything in sight, talk to him before you leave the house. Explain that you will be buying only what is on your list. Tell him that grocery stores are busy places, and you could use a helper. Give him a job to do, such as pushing the cart or helping you empty it at checkout. If he cooperates, you may want to allow him to select one treat or plan a special event (a story or a trip to the park) that you can enjoy together after the shopping is finished. If an incident occurs in the store, remind him of your conversation and redirect his attention. (The problem-solving chapter in Part 2 offers more suggestions.)

Figure 3-3 will help you and your child identify how he or she demonstrates this component of ADD. Add other ways that your child shows his or her impulsivity.

After you have completed the checklist, you may want to look at the strategies for the management of impulsivity described below. Again, begin slowly, and gradually add new ideas as skills develop. Remember, the goal is to develop skills, based on strengths, that will manage the impulsivity for a lifetime. Also, remember to record those strategies that worked successfully and share them with your child's teachers.

1. Use a visual reminder to stop and think.
2. Teach your child to mentally ask "if-then" questions to examine possible results of the actions.
3. Develop organizational skills. Try color coding. Select one color for each subject area. This allows the child to quickly pull materials at the end of the day. Have your child use a daily plan book. Many schools begin to require a plan book by third grade. If your child's teacher does not require a planner, buy one for him anyway. Ask the teacher to check each day's en-

Figure 3–3
Symptoms of Impulsivity

HOME

Constantly reminded to stop and think.
Takes risks that often result in injury.
Interrupts, especially when parent is on the telephone.
Makes poor choices.
Says and does things that cause hurt feelings and often is remorseful.
Makes snap decisions and seldom considers consequences.
Has a difficult time waiting and taking turns.
Transitions are difficult.
More difficult to manage when tired or overstimulated.

SCHOOL

Talks out in class.
Often in trouble because he reacts before considering consequences.
Begins a task before he has all the directions.
Works quickly and is often the first student finished.
Makes "silly" errors that need correcting.
Dislikes going back over work to check for mistakes.
Often states, "I know!" and then needs to ask for more information.
Skips steps and takes shortcuts that interfere with learning.
Difficulty with transitions.
Finds involved, long assignments difficult to manage and complete.

SOCIAL

Doesn't think before speaking, making rude remarks that may hurt friends' feelings.
Often becomes scapegoat.
Easily talked into inappropriate behavior.
Peers annoyed by being frequently interrupted.
Butts into situations, interrupts others' thinking, speaking.
Can't wait turn in games.
Becomes impatient if he has to wait for anything.

---

tries and initial them. A planner can be a great way of communicating with your child's teacher. It should be your child's responsibility to get the signatures each day. A reward system could be put in place if your child meets the expectations.

Large desk calendars are ideal for organizing long-term assignments. If short-term deadlines are not required by the teacher, you and your child should set some. Mark them on the calendar and the child can see the whole project at a glance. By breaking the task down into manageable pieces, it does not appear so overwhelming for the child. If your child is willing, ask the teacher to assign a study buddy. This is a classmate who would assist your child in getting all materials together at the end of the day. Use lists, charts, and schedules to structure your child at home. Remember: If you say it, write it!

4. Give your child choices. This prevents his being overwhelmed by so many selections that he cannot decide, and it eliminates power struggles. Simply state two options and allow your child to decide. For example, "You may either wear this jacket or sweater. You decide." The child knows the weather requires another garment, and he has a limit on his choices. You are not placed in the position of telling him what to wear.

5. Underline, circle, highlight, or in some way indicate key words in directions. Breaking down directions into several numbered steps helps the child to complete all of the assignment. Underlining each step in the directions with a different color helps draw attention to the various steps.

6. Maintain consistency. Changes in the routine can be very disturbing to the child. Make every attempt to limit the number of changes in the daily schedule.

7. Pick your battles. As a family, set three or four house rules. This may help keep you focused on what is really important to enforce and allow the minor incidents to pass.

8. Try contracting. This can be especially effective with older children. With your child, write a contract, listing the terms of the agreement. Keep your expectations realistic and the time limits short. For example, in the beginning, agree to have all homework assignments monitored for completeness each day. This is a more realistic and attainable goal than monitoring on a weekly or monthly basis. Gradually extend time limits as your

child consistently meets each goal. Also define the consequences (try to focus on positive outcomes). Select incentives, such as time alone with Mom or Dad, or an overnight at Grandma's or with a friend. These may be better choices than money, food, or merchandise. Parents and child sign the contract and display it in a place of prominence.

9. Be specific. Requests that imply the child has an option are confusing. "Would you take out the garbage?" is very different from "I want you to empty the garbage."

10. A time-out or quiet place to calm down and regain control can be very helpful.

Putting It All Together

Checklists and strategies provided at the end of the last three sections are to help you, the parents, better understand your child's disorder. It is our hope you will work with your child and his or her teachers to help them understand how his ADD is manifested. It is through continual education and support that your child will begin to learn how to accept responsibility for his or her actions, and how to control them.

Since using ADD as an excuse for misbehavior is never acceptable, learning how to effectively manage the symptoms is essential to success. The symptoms checklists can present a clear picture of the influence of ADD on your child. The strengths sheets, along with a record of the strategies that work effectively, will empower you when you need to advocate for your child.

As a parent, you have the task of finding the child under all the labels. Begin to peel them off one by one. They are there to help you better understand your child. Knowing why your child behaves a certain way will allow you freedom to move on and spend your energy enhancing and developing his strengths.

Neither ADD nor any other disability should ever be used as a crutch or an excuse for inappropriate behavior or failure. If you allow this to happen, your focus remains on what is wrong with your child, and you may never experience all that is right. With just a little searching, parents can find their sensitive, creative, intelligent, humorous child. Focusing on these positive qualities and maintaining a sense of humor allows you to guide your child to a successful future.

Take a few minutes and complete the symptoms-and-strengths balance sheet (Figure 3-6). Include your child in this exercise. It is important for him or her to identify individual strengths. Keep this balance sheet handy and pull it out when you begin to lose focus. Share it with your child often when discouragement and frustration appear. Share it with teachers and ask them to begin using the strengths identified. This balance sheet can serve as a tool to keep the focus on the positive qualities of your child. It will also help you advocate for your child and will be useful in solving problems.

We will provide two examples to get you started. First is Darlene's son Tom, a ninth grader. Tom still struggles with academic problems related to his ADD, but he is learning to discover his strengths as a way to bypass his difficulties. His symptoms-and-strengths sheet is below.

Tom has AD/HD combined type. He is inattentive, hyperactive, and impulsive. He has learned to use his high activity level and his strong gross motor skills to accomplish many tasks. He has several jobs cutting grass. He is mechanically inclined and works on his bike and lawnmowers. After he finishes his jobs, he still has plenty of energy left to fish, swim, and ride his bike around the neighborhood.

Tom has difficulty organizing his work but is very organized with the tools he needs to do the work. He has good visual memory, so visual reminders help him keep focused on his work. Organizing work and information using graphs, charts, and other visuals helps him learn.

Tom also suffers from a low frustration tolerance. When tasks are difficult, he quickly becomes overwhelmed and feels like giving up. This is especially true when he must do large amounts of written work. This is the most difficult symptom for him to manage, because it is intensified by his learning difficulties. He is slowly learning to

Figure 3–4
Tom's Symptoms and Strengths

ADD Symptoms	Strengths
Low frustration tolerence.	Great math skills.
Poor reading comprehension.	Good abstract reasoning skills.
Trouble starting work.	Artistic.
Acts before thinking.	Good gross motor skills.
Poor handwriting.	Good visual memory.
Problems organizing work.	Plays an instrument.
Problems communicating ideas.	Can use a baitcaster.
Fidgets—high activity level.	Can fix lawnmowers.
Trouble staying on task.	Cuts neighbors' grass.
	Builds and flies model rockets.
	Makes friends easily.
	Artistic.
	Good attention to details.
	Very organized with physical objects.
	Plays the guitar.
	Can read and follow a recipe.
	Interested in astronomy.
	Family support.

defuse his frustration through physical activities, such as building model rockets, cooking, fishing, or playing the guitar. These activities are not frustrating for him. These activities build competencies and provide an outlet for the daily frustrations he experiences.

The symptoms of his learning disabilities and AD/HD are still major problems, but they are not insurmountable. Even if his strengths do not eliminate problems, they are more manageable. Plus, knowing his strengths helps him feel good about himself. They protect his spirit. When the spirit is strong, anything is possible!

Tom is still struggling to find his niche in life. Luckily, he is well on his way to developing his strengths into possible avenues for success as an adult. Perhaps his love of fishing will transfer into managing a tackle shop, working on a fishing charter, selling boats, or even being a professional fisherman. His skill in the kitchen might lead him into a career as a professional chef. It could happen!

Nancy's son, Christian, has a balance sheet that looks quite different from Tom's. At twenty-two, Christian has learned to compensate for many of his ADD characteristics, thus minimizing those symptoms that interfered with his learning in elementary and high school. Impulsivity has been the most difficult to control, and remnants of this symptom are still present and are a constant threat.

Pursuing a career in the media, he will be utilizing his strengths and talents in the areas of oral and written communication. The college degree program he is following has very limited math and science requirements, which are his areas of weakness.

Along the way, Christian has learned the skills he will need to live independently as an adult. He has learned to manage and use his ADD as an asset, to the point where he can now maintain a job to finance his college education, assume responsibility for his bills, get to class and work on time, and conduct the everyday business of survival.

Being fiscally responsible is a constant struggle for Christian—one that could result in serious ramifications. He constantly fights the urge to spend, and often, that desire prevails. This is one aspect of Christian's impulsivity difficult to control. To compensate, he often carries a minimal amount of cash and has destroyed his credit cards.

Now that we've given you some samples, sit (or stand, if activity level is an issue for either of you) with your child and complete the balance sheet. Refer back to the symptoms lists to identify problem areas for your children. Include other learning difficulties, such as math or reading problems. The purpose of this exercise is to identify both roadblocks to success and strengths that can become bypass strategies. It is worth repeating: Children change. Children grow and continue to develop strengths, and how ADD-related problems are manifested will change through their life span. Continually update and revise your child's sheet. Remember: Two strengths to every symptom. Be creative.

Figure 3–5
Christian's Symptoms and Strengths

ADD Symptoms	Strengths
Difficulty with math—does not attend to details.	Excellent oral and written communication skills.
Procrastinates—often waits until the last minute to start a project.	Good abstract reasoning skills.
Poor self-monitoring—does not like to go back over things and check work.	Plays the guitar and loves music.
Sleep problems.	Good visual memory.
Impulsive and insatiable spending.	Is empathic.
	Has a good work ethic.
	Assumes responsibility to get to school and work on time.
	Sees the whole picture.
	Creative.
	Great problem-solving skills.
	Makes friends easily.
	Wonderful sense of humor.
	A great negotiator/ peacemaker.
	Individualistic.
	Loyal.
	Strong independent living skills—cooks, does laundry, handles financial responsibilities, etc.
	Loves to read.
	Loves to travel.

How does identifying strengths and weaknesses help you parent the child with ADD?

Step two involves applying this information to understand what is going on in your child's day at school, at home, and with friends. Once you understand what is caused by ADD and what isn't, you can begin building skills, something we will work on in Part 2 of this book.

Figure 3–6
Your Child's Symptoms and Strengths

ADD Symptoms	Strengths

ADD can have a negative impact on every part of your child's life. The same brain goes to school, lives in the family, and plays with friends, so it is understandable that all of these areas can be impacted by the symptoms of ADD. Let's see how that happens.

Describe your child's day. What are the major problems he encounters? How are they related to ADD? Which situations cause the biggest difficulties?

Here's a sample using Tom's balance sheet.

1. At school Tom is always in trouble for chewing on pens and playing with paper clips.
2. He often gets poor marks on written work, because it is illegible and unfinished.

The ADD symptoms causing Tom's school problems are poor handwriting and low frustration tolerance. These contribute to messy work and Tom's giving up on it. It's too frustrating! Tom's high activity level is why he chews on pens and plays with paper clips.

Now that you have seen how this information can be applied, complete your child's personal worksheet (Figure 3-7).

After you have completed this exercise, do the same for home life and social situations. Again, think of times or situations that cause problems or tensions.

Figure 3–7
Your Child's Personal Worksheet

Name two situations causing problems or tension in school.

1. _____

_____

2. _____

_____

How is ADD related to these problems? What symptoms do you see described?

Pick several strengths that could be used to overcome or bypass the above problems. Consider the interventions. Which would be appropriate, considering your child's strengths?

Meeting the Challenge

At this point in our journey together, it should be apparent that there is no easy fix or cure for ADD. What works one day may not work the next. Life becomes a constant challenge to maintain stability and consistency for your child and the rest of the family. Parents feel like they are caught in a traffic jam. Roadblocks and detours are constantly being encountered. It becomes tiring and frustrating trying to progress down the road of life.

As a parent, you know your child best. What your child needs most from you is your unconditional love and acceptance. Your child needs to be respected for *who* he is, not *what* he is. Believing in, and advocating for your child is the greatest gift you can give. If you do not stand up and protect your child's rights, who will?

This is not an easy job when your child has ADD. Parenting a child with ADD can be a tiring, stressful, frustrating, never-ending job. It is a constant struggle to maintain a delicate balance between the home, the school, and the community. You may feel like you are walking a tightrope without a safety net. Even though you still love your child, there are times when you definitely do not like him. At times you may even question whether you love him. It is at these times you need to look past the behavior, see the disorder, and remember the child who is the hardest to love is the child who needs your love the most!

Only with an abundance of hard work, patience, tears and laughter, love and understanding, and a strong support system can you undertake this monumental commitment. As parents who have been traveling down this road for a long time, we can tell you it is worth every minute. Our children are growing and maturing and finding ways to launch themselves successfully in every new adventure.

Below are several suggestions to help you as you detour around your next traffic jam or roadblock.

1. Never use ADD as an excuse for failure or inappropriate behavior. Doing so gives the impression that you are not allowing

your child to accept responsibility for his or her actions.

2. Prioritize your concerns. Top priority is what interferes most with your child's progress. Sometimes it is not the ADD that needs to be addressed first. Emotional or behavioral concerns might take priority. Addressing only one concern at a time is less overwhelming.

3. Try to remain structured and consistent. Set a routine and try to follow it. Establish house rules so the child knows the boundaries. Find phrases or statements to redirect your child, and repeat them often. For example, "That is unacceptable," or "That is inappropriate."

4. Always present a united front. Children can learn very quickly how to divide and conquer to get what they want. Parents need to work together. Single parents may want to ask a friend or relative to offer support and guidance when things get too overwhelming.

5. All caregivers, siblings, and the child need to become educated about ADD. The better you understand the disorder, the less fear you have. The child needs to know that he or she is not alone and having ADD does not mean he or she is dumb or stupid. Becoming informed helps everyone understand the child.

6. Identify your child's strengths. It is on these strengths that his or her education should be built. Careers should be chosen in the areas of strength for optimum success in adulthood.

7. Before you react, step back and count to ten. Then look at the situation carefully and decide if you are seeing misbehavior or the ADD in your child. If you know how ADD affects your child, the appropriate action will follow. Frequent reference to the balance sheet you completed earlier in this section may help you keep your child's symptoms in perspective. Sometimes asking yourself, "What is happening here? Is this the ADD?" can determine what you do next.

8. Create a support team. Pull together all the professionals working with your child and coordinate their efforts to support you and your child.

9. Surround yourself with positive people. Join a parents' support system in your community or school district. Attend regular meetings. Arrange for guest speakers. Share current information. Support groups give parents the opportunity to share their successes and failures. Knowing you are not facing the challenges alone can be very strengthening.

10. Find someone in your child's school who is knowledgeable, understanding, and empathic. Use this person as a buffer between you and your child's teacher.

11. Learn the laws protecting your child's rights and provide for services. Under the Individuals With Disabilities Education Act (IDEA) and Section 504 of the Rehabilitation Act of 1973, the rights of children with ADD are protected. (See Appendix H for the U.S. Department of Education's memorandum.)

12. Learn from your mistakes. Children need to see that parents are human and make errors, too.

13. Laughter truly is the best medicine. It can quickly ease the tension, allowing you to rationally address the situation. Children with ADD do have a unique sense of humor if you just allow yourself to relax and appreciate it.

14. Take time for yourself. Get away, even if only for a ten-minute walk each day. This may sound easier said than done, but try to find someone who can relieve you and allow you time by yourself and with your spouse or friends. This time will help refresh and rejuvenate you.

Hearing that your child is not perfect can be one of the most devastating statements a parent can encounter (especially dads!). However, anger and denial are nonproductive and only delay getting help and assistance for you and your child. The information offered in this part of the book hopefully has made the acceptance of your child's disorder less intimidating and overwhelming. We have offered some tools to help you and your child begin to understand the ADD and see it as a strength rather than a weakness.

The diagnosis of attention deficit disorders does not make your child any less appealing. If anything, it has opened a whole new world of possibilities. With your guidance and direction, your child could be the world's newest inventor, composer, artist, statesperson, author, philosopher, researcher, or educator. The possibilities are endless! Einstein's and Edison's parents believed in them, and look what they accomplished.

PART TWO

Building Skills for Competence

4

Communication

Almost everyone has played the game "telephone." You start with a simple story or phrase which is repeated around the circle. Usually by the time the story gets back to the beginning, it is distorted. The meaning of the story may be changed or facts omitted. Pretty funny when it's a game. Not so funny when you are communicating for real with friends, spouses, teachers, or your children.

Talking and listening: Pretty simple words but not very simple actions. We talk and our listener doesn't have the foggiest idea what we're trying to say. We listen and we swear they are talking in a foreign language. Are we talking about the same situation? That is not how I saw it or what I heard. How do we get so confused?

Communication is much more than speaking words and listening to others' words. Communication involves postures, facial expressions, and gestures. It involves interpreting, reflecting, and responding.

The authors of *Connecting with Self and Others* describe four basic styles of communications, based on the work of William F. Hill. Style one includes small talk and shop talk. Style two is control talk, spite, or fight talk. Style three is search talk, and the final style is straight talk. Below is a greatly simplified explanation of the uses and purposes of each style of communication.

Small talk serves the purpose of letting others know information about yourself. It helps build rapport with others. Children with ADD may find this type of communication very difficult. They may be great at giving information about themselves but unable to sense nonverbal clues indicating their talking partner wishes to change the subject or is offended or upset by something they have said. Shop talk focuses on work-related messages. For children, this means discussing homework with the teacher or peers and asking which day the history test will take place or who won Friday's football game.

Control talk might better be called take-charge talking. The purpose here is to gain agreement, not to force compliance. When used correctly, control talk can direct children, set limits, and positively reinforce behaviors. The statement "Your room needs cleaning. Let's set up a plan and a time to clean out those cupboards, so you have more room for your things," tells children what needs to be done and encourages agreement, because it is not judgmental. Suggestions are offered and an understanding conveyed of why it has been difficult to complete the task (there is no room in the closet).

When used ineffectively, control talk can lead to resentment. Excessive use of control talk can lead to what the authors call "fight or spite." The goal here is not to gain agreement but to send negative or destructive or shaming messages. Fight talk is characterized by "you" messages. The sender often wants to avoid responsibility and get his way through blaming, attacking, threatening, putting down others, or listening defensively. "I don't want to hear it! Your room is a pig sty, and you are the biggest slob I ever saw. I can't wait until you are gone." How would you react? You're not likely to gain acceptance or persuade using this method.

Search talk provides an opportunity to clarify situations, brainstorm ideas, or reflect on what you think others are saying. This style of communication is marked by open-ended questions and phrases or words such as *what if* and *possibility*. The mood here is calm, supportive, and inquisitive. This is a perfect style of communication for teacher-parent conferences or when trying to solve problems with your child. Search talk avoids power struggles, supplies information, and provides a great model of effective communication.

The final style of communicating is straight talk. Straight talk is acknowledging your own reality, what you are seeing, thinking, and feeling. This style can communicate both negative and positive feelings or thoughts. Straight talk is open and honest, but respectful and tactful. The goal isn't to persuade others to think as you do but to communicate your reality. This talk is marked by "I" statements linked with your feelings, thoughts, or wants, e.g., "I am very frustrated by the mess in your room."

Why is communication important? Ineffective communication can lead to power struggles, hurt feelings, and frustration. Effective communication can increase the probability of getting your needs, wants, and rights—as well as those of your child—respected and met.

It is important for you to communicate effectively not only with your child but also with professionals such as physicians and teachers.

All these styles of communication are used by each of us. The decision to use each style might be unconscious. But as we become more aware of how we communicate, we can use this knowledge to increase the likelihood of our goals being met.

We don't recommend using spite or fight talk as a way of getting you or your child's needs met. We do bet you will encounter, on occasion, this style of communication. Understanding where the speaker is coming from prepares you to defuse the situation.

Communicating is a circular process. We speak verbally and nonverbally. Our listener processes this information, and if our verbal and nonverbal messages are congruent, he most likely receives the intended message. If our verbal and nonverbal information do not match, the listener will likely be confused.

Researcher Albert Mehrabian, Ph.D., started the study of communication years ago with these findings: visual messages account for 55 percent of what is received and believed in spoken communication. The way you deliver a message vocally accounts for 38 percent. What is actually said accounts for a mere 7 percent.

There are many factors besides conflict between verbal and non-verbal messages that allow communication to fall apart. Communication is a cycle, and the results depend not just on whether the visual message is congruent with the auditory one. How effectively the listener processes information is also important. As listeners we may find it difficult to understand or assimilate all the information we receive. Have you ever left a teacher-parent conference and started to recap what was discussed only to discover you didn't understand or couldn't remember much of it?

In this section we will focus on developing effective communication skills. The goals are to enhance your ability to reach and teach your child and to assist you in communicating with the professionals who are working with him.

Communication is a skill, and as with many of the skills our children need, there are roadblocks to competency.

Parent-Child Communication

Wouldn't it be wonderful if every time we made a request our kids fulfilled it? Homework done on our schedule. Clothes picked up the first time. Fat chance, you say? OK, you are right. It's only a dream. Life isn't like that, especially if you have a child with ADD.

Interacting with children isn't easy. What brings a response from one child may lead to fight talk from another. There is no recipe guaranteeing perfection every time. Add to the volatile mix a parent and child who are both impulsive or hyperactive and conversation can quickly become fireworks. It's not a pretty sight.

There are things parents can do to facilitate a good relationship and communication with their children. As we effectively communicate with our children, we are actually modeling skills they need.

Change "you" to "I" and "don't" to "do"

A very humbling experience might be to make an audiotape of a day or afternoon of conversations with your child. How often would you hear yourself say things like the following: *Stop. No. You know better. Didn't you hear me? What did I say? Are you deaf? Shut up. Be quiet. I'm going to count to three. You never listen. If I've told you once I've told you a hundred times.* Are you blushing yet? If this sounds all too familiar, don't despair. These statements are roadblocks to good communication, but that doesn't mean we leave them in the road. We can learn a new pattern of talking and reroute or repair relationships damaged by poor communication. By now you have figured out that it does not work well to adopt the drill-sergeant method of parent-child communication. The best solution is to develop a new frame of reference.

A great way to start is by making "I" messages a part of your communications. "I" messages encourage listening. They are brief, consistent messages that focus on your thoughts or feelings about the subject. Avoid "you" messages that condemn, judge, or place your child on the defensive.

There is a direct connection between the way children feel and the way they act. Be sure to acknowledge your child's frame of reference or feelings when communicating. Denying feelings can shut down communication and lead to fights.

CHILD: You're mean. You never let me camp in the woods with the other kids.

PARENT: I'm sorry you feel that way. I don't think it's safe to stay in the woods at night.

CHILD: Everybody else's mom lets them stay in the woods.

PARENT: I am sure it seems like all the other parents let their children spend the night in the woods, but we have to do what we think is safe and right for you.

In the above conversation the child is allowed to convey his feelings, and his frustration is acknowledged. The parent defuses a potential power struggle or an escalation of the situation to fight talk by using "I" statements to indicate she has heard what the child said, and reinforced her position by providing information.

CHILD: You're mean. You never let me spend the night in the woods like the other kids.

PARENT: I don't care what the other kids do, you are not spending the night in the woods.

CHILD   You're mean. I hate you.

PARENT: No, you don't. Only bad kids talk like that to their parents.

CHILD: I don't care what you say.

PARENT: Don't be so ungrateful. After all we have done for you, you act like this.

This is communication gone wrong, talk turned to fighting, spite talk, and power struggle. The child's feelings are not acknowledged ("I don't care what the other kids do"). Feelings are denied ("No, you don't"). Finally, the parent loses control of the conversation, falling into spite talk and sending negative "you" messages of judgment to the child ("you are ungrateful" and "Only bad kids talk like that").

Another reason we don't receive compliance from our children is that we are constantly telling them what *not* to do. Don't eat with food in your mouth. Don't run. Don't touch that. Don't tap that pencil. Don't doodle. Don't fidget. We expect actions to stop, but we provide no alternatives.

Can you think of alternative "do" statements for the above? Do walk. Do tap the pencil's eraser instead of the point. Doodle on the paper, not on the book. Do eat with your mouth shut. "Do" statements teach instead of condemn.

Triple-A roadblocks:
assumptions, assimilation, awareness

There are three *As* to consider when talking with children with ADD. Ignoring these considerations is a sure-fire way to end up mired in a swamp of misunderstanding.

Fact one:

You can't *assume* anything. Never assume your child knows or understands your point of view, what you are talking about, or from where you're coming. It is entirely possible for two people to carry on a conversation, think they know what the other said, and be completely wrong.

Children with ADD often possess a wonderful trait called free flight of ideas. You tell your child, "We are going to get ice cream after we go to the park, so be sure to bring clean shoes and socks." Immediately, he begins taking a mind journey about previous adventures in the park, imagining the tadpoles in the pond and dragonflies scooting across the water.

Hours later, you leave the park and remind him to put on his clean shoes and socks. "What socks and shoes? You never told me to bring them." Never assume he *received* the message. Ask for an instant replay to verify that the message got through.

Fact two:

Kids with ADD often do not *assimilate* information. Repeat key instructions and ask for clarification to ensure not only the entire message, but that the *meaning* of your message was finally conveyed. Did your child take in all the required information? What did he miss? Even when children get the message, they might find it difficult to use information in a constructive manner. What does your child think you meant by your message, and what should he do to convey assimilation?

Fact three:

Children with ADD may lack an *awareness* of what is happening around them. It is not that they willfully disregard what is happening. They don't notice. Their world is moving too quickly. They miss valuable communications or may be unaware of the meaning of expressions or changes in the tone of voice.

Helping your child become aware of nonverbal clues can be a challenge. He may have difficulty paying attention to small details such as facial expressions or speech patterns. Try practicing these skills by role playing or by playing charades. Make the expressions outrageous in the beginning so that it is obvious what is happening. "How Are You Feeling Today?" Posters or T-shirts also help to raise awareness. Remember: Never assume. Ask kids to name the feeling or expression.

Another suggestion is to speak from behind a mask and have your child decide if your voice matches what you are saying. What feeling is your voice suggesting? Is that what your words say? Again, in the beginning, exaggerate the voices so it is obvious what is happening. For the child still having difficulty understanding these clues, you might ask what it was that made him think you were angry or happy or sad.

Things to look for:

- Changes in facial muscles. Have the eyes or mouth changed?
- Check out the lower lip. What would a grimace mean? What does biting on the lip mean?
- Changes in skin color. Is the person you are speaking to turning bright red? Not a good sign.
- Changes in the rate of speech. If people are nervous or anxious to be understood, they may speak more rapidly. Hesitation or broken speech may indicate the speaker lacks confidence or is hesitant about relaying information.
- Changes in volume of speech. Increased loudness may indicate frustration or a need to persuade or gain agreement.
- Nonverbal clues can confirm what words mean. It is also important not to read too much into them. A person may speak loudly because he has a hearing problem. His skin may flush because

the room is hot. If he is hyperactive, he might naturally speak quickly.

Mapping the road for good communication

Like every journey, communication starts somewhere. Establishing a starting point lets kids know you are available. Try modeling the following behavior to signal to your child that you are available and willing to communicate.

- Pay careful attention. Let your child know that what he is saying is important to you. When your child comes home from school with his latest artwork or math test, don't respond with a short glance and a "That's nice." Take a moment to carefully observe the work and comment on the effort needed to complete it. Ask how your child got the idea for the art or how he likes math.
- Use a soft voice when talking to your child. Kathy Enos, parent of a child with ADD, says she uses her FM radio voice. When she needs to communicate something important, she speaks in a soft, firm voice and uses straight talk. This method teaches children how to communicate honestly without anger. In the beginning, this may be difficult for many of us. We might have grown up in families where communication often consisted of angry yelling. No news was good news, and getting a talking to meant you were in deep trouble. It takes time to change these patterns. With time and practice, finding your FM voice becomes second nature.
- Avoid talking down to your child, and don't hide the truth as you know it. Sometimes adults think children are too young, too immature to understand. Young people have a great way of letting parents know when they've done this. A blank stare and a "duh" get the message across—their way. Kids can handle what they know. What that means is that secrets and the unknown are harder to handle. Children with ADD or learning difficulties may feel dumb or stupid. They need straight talk from parents

to help them understand their strengths. In the beginning of this book, you developed a balance sheet and a strength sheet. Use those sheets as starting points for conversation. Help your child understand where he stands.

Major no-nos

Don't get historic or hysterical. Avoid going to pieces or going down Memory Lane. It never helps to bring up the test they failed last year or the fight they got into in first grade.

We'll give you a grace period of a few days. If your child is in trouble because a problem-solving strategy developed days ago failed, it's OK to review the problem behavior, why the strategy didn't work, or what the new strategy should be. But the reasonable rule is to deal with the here and now. Dealing or focusing on past incidents takes the focus away from the current problem. Bringing up old problems doesn't motivate kids to change. It may reinforce their low self-esteem and leave them believing it is hopeless and they can't do anything right.

Parents' time-out

It's been a bad day. The kids are fighting. The teacher called, and the car died. You are ready to either pull out your hair or trade your child for a hound dog, maybe both. Take a time-out. You owe it to yourself to take time to collect your thoughts. It's not reasonable to expect parents to be emotionally ready to deal with every crisis on a moment's notice.

When things go wrong, it's OK to say, "I don't know what I'm going to do." Model taking time out and the STAR concept of stopping, thinking, and reflecting on what happened before making decisions.

This gives kids time to think about what happened. We admit it may seem contrary to setting limits and clear consequences. However, sometimes things happen or circumstances indicate handling matters differently. We need structure and we need to be flexible. Use these teachable moments to help children understand that sometimes things aren't black and white, and all sides of a situation must be considered in order to make good decisions.

It's OK to let kids know you are angry or upset and can't make a decision. Explain you need time out to calm down. Tell children the decision is too important to make lightly and you need time and a clear head to make a fair decision.

One factor that will determine how parents react is their ability to discern what is going on under the surface. What is your child trying to communicate through actions that he can't express in words?

Try not to react to circumstances, but determine what is happening. Resolve not to get personal by using fight or spite talk. Use the information you gain during your time out to make an informed, controlled decision.

Family meetings

During our hectic days, situations often come up that can't be resolved in a few moments. Siblings fight over chores or complain about unfair treatment. These problems are ideal topics for family meetings.

In order to gain your child's cooperation, set up ground rules for family talk time. First make meeting times agreeable to everyone. Give everyone advance notice. Let your family make up their own ground rules. We encourage rules like "No put downs" and "No idea is a bad idea." Children also need permission to pass if they don't feel like talking. When someone talks, everyone has to listen, and one person should talk at a time, without interruptions.

Family meetings need to be safe places to communicate. Let children say what they feel. Acknowledge feelings and agree that it's OK to disagree. Make using "I" messages mandatory.

A family meeting is a great opportunity to set family rules and consequences. It should be established that anything can be brought to the table and discussed. Until children are convinced that the meeting is a safe activity, you might not get much participation. If this happens, start with small problems, and enlist the family members to help you solve them. Follow the problem-solving model in the next section to determine your plan. The beauty is that no plan has to be final or permanent. If a plan doesn't work, it can always be brought back to the table.

Compliance Through Communication

Angry, frustrated children are a challenge to any parent. It would be unrealistic to think we aren't going to have power struggles, arguments, and confused conversations. The best we can do is try to defuse explosive situations and deal with them as adults when they occur.

It is important for us to look for clues from children that will indicate their perspective and their needs. When your child is out of control, the goal is not to control her but to help her gain self-control.

Children with ADD may have very little internal control. Hyperactivity or impulsivity may override the little internal control they possess. The suggestions in part one can help you help your child deal with these issues without destroying her self-esteem.

When compliance is a problem, describe (using your FM voice and "I" statements) the exact behavior at issue. State why the behavior is a problem and how you feel about it. Finally, let your child know what action you would like her to take to change the situation. Pause and let the child think about what you have said.

If a time-out is appropriate, prescribe one for your child, or take one yourself. When it is over, remind your child that you love her but do not like the behavior and cannot accept it. Talk about what happened and how it can be avoided in the future.

Can't or won't

Often we make the assumption that a child is refusing to comply simply out of stubbornness when in fact he is being asked to do something he literally can't do. Look at the task and ask yourself if your requests are appropriate. Did you send your child to his room with a simple "Clean it up"? Did he know what to do first and where to put things? Did you set your child up for failure by not providing clear, concise instructions?

Kids' time-out

Time-out is beneficial to kids too. Time out gives parent and child space and everyone time to cool off. When a child is given time out, the reason should be explained to the child. "That behavior is not acceptable. Go to time-out. When you are under control, come back and we will talk about what happened." Children should be encouraged to take their own time-out when they feel they are on the verge of losing control. In the home, a safe place should be defined, a place where the child can gather his emotions. Parents sometimes use stairs, an open hall, or a space under the table. Sending a child to his room is fine if his room isn't like Toys 'R Us.

Children need to know it's OK to be angry. The challenge is to find a safe and appropriate way to release the anger. Hitting others, breaking toys, or cursing is not acceptable.

Decide in your family meetings what is acceptable behavior, what the consequences of misbehaving will be, and where time-outs will be spent. Although we might enjoy it, the idea is not to send our child to his room for the duration. It is to give him breathing room. The recommended time is one minute for each year of the child's age. Kids should be given the option of staying in time-out until they are under control and ready to review what happened.

Older kids might decide to stay in time-out as a way of punishing us (it's oh-so-painful!). "I'm not coming out and talking to you," John yells from his room. "That's OK. When you feel ready to talk, come on out," Mom replies.

Some children with ADD may be emotionally exhausted by their own outbursts. Johnny might slam his door, throw himself on his bed and cry, and then take a nap. After all the negative energy and frustration is spent, he is able to reflect on what happened and find ways of avoiding future problems.

Self-discipline

As unpleasant as it is for parents, a child's lack of self-control is even more frightening to the child. Children with ADD are often blind-sided by their quick frustration, impulsiveness, or hyperactivity. They continually react in ways they don't understand, which further frustrates them. Sometimes we're amazed at the seeming insignificance of the problem that sets our off child. Discerning parents soon learn what will trigger their child's impulsiveness or temper.

This knowledge can lead to more teachable moments. Triggers are red flags that problems are about to occur. For younger children, your intervention might be necessary. Older children can learn to identify these, but be warned it's not an easy task. We are talking years. For some, these problems are lifelong struggles.

Children show their feelings by acting out. No one objects if those feelings are happy. We all love getting a hug or a kiss or listening to our child sing.

When feelings are unhappy and the actions are unhealthy the problems begin. Since all feelings are OK, it only makes sense to help children distinguish between healthy and unhealthy ways of sharing feelings and to understand the consequences of those actions.

To help children identify the relationships between feelings, actions, and consequences, fill out the following chart (Figure 4-1). Several sections have been completed to get you started. Are any actions both healthy and unhealthy? When would they be healthy and when not? The goal of the activity is to help children identify whether an action is healthy or not, what feeling might go with an action, and what the consequences might be.

When was the last time your child lost control or acted out feelings in an unhealthy way? Discuss the consequences of these actions with your child and brainstorm alternative ways of acting.

Figure 4–1
Actions and Consequences Chart

FEELING	ACTION	HEALTHY/ UNHEALTHY	CONSEQUENCES
happy	hug someone	healthy	share happiness
	dance		
	yell		
sad	cry	healthy	feel better
	laugh		
nervous	bite your nails	unhealthy	sore fingertips
	get even		
	exercise		
	hit someone		
	talk to someone		
	sleep		
	scream		
	throw things		
	clean your room		
	smoke		
	beat your pillow		
	write it down		
	listen to music		
	kiss someone		
	hide out		
	go jogging		
	give up		
	sing		
	garden		
	skip school		
	take a nap		
	break something		
	wash a window		
	trip someone		

Autonomy-versus-power rules

We don't see the value in corporal punishment for children, especially those with ADD. We realize there are many who think our kids would benefit from a swift kick across the behind and a few other places. That is an old paradigm and contradicts what we hope our children will do.

Impulsive or aggressive children need to be taught control. Corporal punishment may solve the problem for the moment, but what does it teach? We think it encourages aggression by teaching that the most powerful or aggressive person will be obeyed. We have personally seen children use these tactics to resolve problems with peers. Using strength over reason only sets up the child for more problems and doesn't teach how to avoid them.

As parents we have to decide what we stand for. Do we want to teach our children power rules and that those in authority will be obeyed at all cost? Some of you may be nodding your head in agreement and thinking "You're darn right we do." We think a little rebellion is OK.

We want to teach our children to self-govern, to have self-control, and to be autonomous—not to be lambs led to the slaughter. We aren't advocating letting children defy parents or teachers or police officers. But they have a basic right to a guided self-determination.

When your child stomps his feet and yells "It's not fair!" you might be inclined to inform him "Life isn't fair." Please stop for a moment before you do. Ask your child why it's not fair and help him to see the incident or decision from another point of view. Children often think in black-and-white terms: This is right, that is wrong, and there's no in-between.

Many things in life are not fair. It is important for our children to accept this. But there are also many unfair things that we can change. It is important to realize that, too.

Some schools have a policy of group punishment. If one child acts out at recess or in the classroom, the entire class gets indoor recess or written punishments. The injustice for the child with ADD, who is often on the receiving end of these punishments, is too much to endure. Being denied recess because your work is messy or sitting against the wall at lunch because you can't sit still in class isn't fair. Would we punish a child who had seizures in the classroom?

Sending your child to his room with the pronouncement "Life isn't fair" and a swat across the bottom might feel good and resolve the problem for the moment. But what has it taught your child? Help your child learn to communicate her frustration in a healthy way. Be a sounding board for your child's frustration. Then you have taught a valuable lesson.

Child-to-Child Communication

Learning to communicate with peers is an important part of developing as a social person. Children must learn how to listen to other children as well as what to say. Many children are unsure how to approach other children or what to say when they meet them.

Begin by helping your child learn small talk or shop talk. Role play in different situations, such as calling a classmate on the phone and asking what homework is due for the night.

Teach good telephone manners. How do you ask for someone on the phone? Introduce yourself. Ask for the person with whom you wish to speak. Thank the person who answered the phone. It is even helpful to have tips written on note cards when the child is first learning these skills.

Another problem may be having friends over. Provide a script for your child detailing how to welcome their guest.

- Say hello.
- Ask your friend what he would like to do.
- Offer suggestions.
- Take turns. Don't monopolize the conversation.
- Ask questions.

Teach your child words and body language to encourage other children to speak. Nodding the head or smiling indicates interest in what the other person is saying. Words such as "uh-huh," "I see," "OK," and "wow," encourage the speaker to continue. These seem like such simple ideas, and they are. But the child with ADD may need practice to become proficient at small talk. Practice these scripts with your child and he will be more at ease when friends come over or he meets new people.

Child-to-Teacher Communication

When surveyed, teachers indicated that one of the most common aggravations they encountered in teaching was the student who responds, "Huh? I don't get it." Nothing is more infuriating to an educator who has just given a twenty-minute explanation.

Teachers do not have a problem with the fact that the child does not understand. The annoyance occurs because the child is not specific about where the confusion arises. When asked, "What is it you don't understand?" the student usually responds, "I don't get any of it."

Rarely do children have a complete lack of understanding of what is being said. Usually there is a portion of the conversation that has caused confusion. What often occurs is that the child may not know how to ask for clarification to resolve the confusion. Explaining where the breakdown in understanding has occurred is often difficult for the child to do. Therefore, you may need to backtrack through the explanation. "Do you understand how we got the number 4 in the quotient?" "Yes, you divided 4 into 17." "Good! What do we do next?" It is often necessary to proceed through the process step-by-step until the specific point of breakdown is identified.

At home, you can help your child learn how to ask clarification questions. The next time he announces, "I don't get it!" have him try to explain specifically which part he does not understand. Remind him that neither you nor the teacher can help him unless he tries to make the source of the problem clear. Help him learn to methodically go through the process until he arrives at the point where the confusion occurs.

When the Communication Cycle Breaks Down: ADD Plus

While many children become very competent at using language to communicate information, maintain a conversation in social situations, read the nonverbal cues of those around them, and get their needs met, a significant number of children have a "break" in their language cycle. Children who have a language impairment may appear to have ADD when in reality they cannot keep up with the pace of the conversation. To further complicate the issue, many children diagnosed with ADD may also have a language processing disability. This can be one of the comorbid, or related, disabilities of ADD. Sorting out the two disorders takes the involvement of experienced professionals.

If the child has ADD, it may be the symptoms of the disorder which are interfering with the child's ability to process and use information. In order to talk effectively with someone, maintaining eye contact and focusing on what the other person is saying and doing are very important. For inattentive, impulsive children with ADD, this can be a very difficult task. They often jump ahead without getting all the information they need, or they constantly interrupt, which proves to be very annoying and disturbing to the communication partner.

Because the child's disorder gets in the way of listening to what is being said, he also misses the nonverbal cues being sent by the other person. For example, Johnny is playing tag on the playground. The game is getting too rough, and the other children want to do something else. Johnny is so caught up in the adventure, he does not hear that the others have had enough, nor does he read the irritation and anger they are beginning to show. It requires the involvement of an adult or a scuffle with a peer to get Johnny under control. The result is that Johnny is in trouble again and has alienated himself further from the group from which he wants acceptance. This scenario can describe a child who has ADD, a pragmatic language disability, or both.

There are several places where communication can break down. If any of these areas to be described reminds you of your child, you may want to contact your school's speech and language pathologist and request a comprehensive language evaluation to see if your child qualifies for services.

Pragmatic language

Pragmatic language is the way language is used in everyday conversation. Gestures, humor, body language, dialects, and slang are examples of pragmatic language. Being aware of others' feelings by translating facial expressions and tones of voice are other facets of this form of language usage.

The example given above demonstrates what can occur if the child has a problem with pragmatic language. Johnny did not understand the meaning of no when his peers wanted to stop playing tag. He was not aware of the anger and frustration on their faces and in their voices when they told him to stop pursuing them. He saw humor and playfulness in a situation where those qualities no longer existed.

Respecting the "personal space" of other people is another aspect of pragmatic language. Many children with a pragmatic language disability will enter this personal zone and get in the faces of their peers, not realizing this causes the other children to feel intimidated and uncomfortable. This further distances the child with the disability.

Another area where a pragmatic language disability may cause problems is misunderstanding the feelings others have toward the child. Laughter interpreted as someone laughing at him rather than with him may cause self-esteem issues, and the child may begin to withdraw and refuse to take risks, or he may lash out with anger and frustration. Becoming the class clown is one way a child looking for peer acceptance may behave. This child is also at risk because other children often "set up" the child and use him as a scapegoat. Classmates often get great pleasure watching the innocent lamb go to the slaughter.

Social registering is the ability to adjust the use of verbal and nonverbal language to match the person or situation encountered. Often children with a pragmatic language disability will address the teacher or principal in the same manner and with the same vocabulary they use with their peers. They do not understand that speaking to adults requires a more respectful tone of voice, a different choice of words (street language and slang are not appropriate), and a stance of looking alert and attentive. When children lack this awareness and do not make the appropriate switch from situation to situation, they appear to be mouthy, arrogant, and disrespectful when, in fact, they may have a pragmatic language disability.

Strategies you may want to try with your child are listed below. Through role-play, give your child the opportunity to practice the intervention most comfortable for him before he tries to apply it.

1. Respecting personal space.

    Have your child observe the distance people keep between themselves. Point out that strangers are farther apart than parents or relatives. Discuss that any touching of the other person depends on the relationship. For example, parents and relatives you would readily hug or touch, but strangers or acquaintances might just shake hands.

    Help your child learn to recognize the signs when he has violated the space of another—such signs as leaning away or stepping back, pushing, and looks of discomfort (grimacing, frowning). Demonstrate different facial expressions and body movements. Have him recognize how he reacts when someone gets too close.

    Place a measuring tape or draw a chalk line on the ground. Ask your child to stand at one end. Describing someone at the other end (parent, teacher, friend), ask your child to walk the line and stop where he thinks an appropriate distance from that person would be.

2. Developing awareness of nonverbal messages.

    Videotaping can be a very useful tool. Tape your child, a sibling, other children, or a TV program. Watch the tape with the sound turned off. Stop the tape and ask your child to identify and interpret facial expressions, gestures, and body postures that he sees.

Tape a TV program and view it with the sound off. Ask your child to give an interpretation of what is occurring based on the facial expressions and body language. Ask him to focus on one character and describe how that actor is feeling. Stop the tape and ask your child to predict what will happen next.

Using a video camera or a mirror, ask your child to demonstrate various feelings. Do his facial expressions match the feeling? Does he look angry, scared, or happy?

Role-play situations that evoke a range of expressions, gestures, and body posture—receiving a new bike, for example, or missing the goal at a soccer game, or breaking a neighbor's window. Discuss the expressions of the recipients of the actions.

There are many posters available displaying facial expressions of human emotions. Some are even printed on T-shirts. Purchasing or making such a poster may be helpful in developing awareness.

3. Developing a social register.

Through role-play, practice the postures, facial expressions, tones of voice, and words to use in different situations—for example, when talking to Grandma, a neighbor, a friend, a clergyman, a police officer, the librarian, or a principal. Videotaping may again be helpful.

Receptive language disability

A child with a receptive language disability often has difficulty understanding spoken language. When too much is presented at one time, the child goes on auditory overload and shuts down. Following directions, especially those with two or more steps, can be very difficult for this child. A firm understanding of such directional concepts as "over," "under," "beneath," "beside," or "on top of" is not always established. He may not see the humor in a joke, a pun, or a play on words. He may laugh because everyone else is but without understanding why. Words with abstract or multiple meanings also pose a problem for children with a receptive language disability. This can interfere with the child's understanding of what is read.

In the classroom, information should be presented in a variety of ways. This child learns best by seeing and doing, and providing such opportunities will greatly reduce reliance on auditory information.

Because this child gets overwhelmed easily by too much oral information at one time, teachers need to offer ways to accommodate the child.

1. Allow the child to record lectures or extensive instructions on tape. The child can then go back over the information at her own pace. Provide personal notes for the child to follow and use during the lecture and instructional time. Provide a "note buddy." Have the child take notes but supplement those notes with those of another student willing to share. In some classrooms, carbon paper is used to make copies of peer notes. These notes are put in a binder available in the classroom for any child to use.

2. Asking students to repeat back instructions using their own words allows the teacher to check for understanding and give the child who is processing slowly another opportunity to hear the same message again in another way.

3. At home, monitor the speed with which you speak to this child. Speaking too quickly and giving rapid-fire instructions can be very overwhelming. Slow down and give your child an opportunity to process what you are saying.

4. Providing written instructions may eliminate the need for your child to process and retain too much information at once. Supplement your oral information with notes or model the things you want accomplished.

Before giving the child directions, call his name to get his attention. Then ask him to watch your eyes and maintain eye contact while the instructions are being given. Next, check for understanding by asking your child to repeat back to you, in his own words, what he is supposed to do.

As mentioned, many children with ADD also have a receptive language disability. However, many children who appear to be ADD are truly language impaired. When their brains go on auditory overload, they drift off and appear very distracted. Therefore, it is very important to look carefully at the warning signs for each disability and consult with a professional to get an accurate diagnosis.

Expressive language disability

Expressive language involves the brain's ability to organize information it receives and prepare a written or oral response. Many children with an expressive language disability give delayed responses that have nothing to do with the current topic of conversation. Many cannot find the words or sequence thoughts quickly enough to express how they are feeling. For this reason, they will overuse "er," "uh," and other fillers while they are trying to process. Because they have difficulty verbally expressing themselves, many children get frustrated and demonstrate their strong feelings through inappropriate behavior.

Rambling is another common characteristic of this disorder. Coming to the point is very difficult, because organizing thoughts to deliver information in a systematic manner is part of the disability. The child's mind is flitting from one idea to the next, causing the listener to become confused and impatient. Information is often out of sequence, and the overuse of pronouns or vague references adds to this confusion. The listener can get worn out just trying to follow the line of thought and make sense of the jumble.

Children with an expressive language disability will often focus on the insignificant aspects rather than on what is important. To these children, everything is of equal importance. On a trip to the firehouse, the pencil on the fireman's desk is just as important as sitting on the fire engine. In reading a passage, finding the main idea is difficult because to them everything in the paragraph or story is equally important.

The following ideas may help ease the stress on children trying to communicate:

- Give the gift of time. At home and at school, give the child an opportunity to respond. Teachers may ask a question and erase the board or put away a book, thus providing a "wait time" while the students formulate their answers. At home, give the same processing time after asking a question.
- Teachers may have a secret signal for the child and use it to cue the child before it is his turn to respond.
- Reading aloud may be difficult and embarrassing for the child. Silent reading may be more productive and less stressful.
- Maintaining a consistent routine may be very helpful. The constant stress of trying to make sense of language can be very tiring. Knowing the routine and expectations can be an energy saver.

Written language disability

Some children may have well-developed oral skills that mask or compensate for their poor writing skills. Allow us to clarify immediately what is meant by poor writing skills. This does not always mean a lack of pencil control or fine motor skills. Fine motor skills involve the coordination and precision of the body's smaller muscles, like those found in the hand and used in the actual writing process.

Young children, given opportunities in preschool and kindergarten, to use, exercise, and develop the muscles in the hand, usually have the coordination to master pencil control by the end of first grade. Children who are past that point and still find writing tasks difficult and frustrating may be experiencing a written language disability.

Fine motor control is just a small part of the writing process. For you to write a sentence, several things must occur. First, you have to think of what you want to say. Then that thought must be organized and the words put in the correct order to have your idea make sense. Next you have to hold that thought in your head long enough to transfer it to paper. In order to make that transfer, you have to remember how to form each letter in the word and the sequence of the letters so the words are spelled correctly. Awareness of line and space in positioning each letter on the paper is very important. Beginning with a capital letter and ending each sentence with a period or a question mark is also part of the process—not to mention all the commas and other punctuation needed within the sentence. And you thought you just picked up a pencil or pen and began writing! The writing process is very complicated and requires the coordination of many brain functions all at once. Add to this complex process the rapidly moving, often distracted brain of the child with ADD and you may begin to understand why dysgraphia (a written language disability) and ADD often go hand in hand.

Writing can be a slow and painful procedure for the child. Dysgraphia is often characterized by a resistance to writing anything. For the child with this impairment, writing assignments often consist of short, simplistic sentences. An essay or answer on a test may consist of one or two sentences. This may indicate not how much the child knows but how much he is able to produce.

Taking notes can result in incomplete information, for two reasons. First, the child may not hear the information. Then, the brain may not make sense of it quickly enough for the child to be able to write down what needs to be remembered. If writing is slow and inefficient, few notes may be recorded because the child gets lost in the process and shuts down in frustration.

Therefore, many accommodations may need to be made, especially as the child gets older and is expected to write more and more.

1. To strengthen and develop fine motor muscles, clay or dough, fat pencils and crayons, lacing cards, Legos, and tracing, cutting and pasting activities are helpful.
2. Develop your child's keyboarding skills early. Begin young chil-

dren not on a computer but on a typewriter, because they need to press the keys harder, so the fine motor muscles are getting more exercise. Later, move the child to the computer keyboard. (If you do not have a typewriter available, contact local businesses or schools that are updating their technology. They might also be able to offer you a good deal on a used computer.) Mavis Beacon is the name of a computer software package that teaches keyboarding skills at several different age and skill levels.

3. Once keyboarding skills are in place, request that the teacher accept all written work completed on the typewriter or computer. Most teachers prefer this accommodation for students with poor handwriting skills. For the child, it is a much easier and efficient way to complete assignments, and the final copy is much neater.

4. Request that your child be allowed to complete in-class essays or essay tests in the school's computer lab. Experience shows that children who are thus accommodated produce more information, get a higher grade, and are prouder of the appearance of the finished product.

5. Oral testing may be a reliable alternative for the child with a handwriting disability. This is especially effective for the child with strong verbal skills. Many teachers who test orally are amazed at the amount of knowledge a student has but cannot produce in writing.

6. For long essay tests or exams, teachers may want to consider giving the student with handwriting difficulties a modified test or require him to answer two out of four questions. This has been done effectively and discreetly by teachers in many classrooms.

7. Two grades may be given on written assignments—one for content and the other for grammar, spelling, and punctuation. Or the teacher may grade for content and allow grammatical and spelling errors.

8. Refer back to the suggestions given under the receptive-lan-

guage-disability section earlier in this chapter for ways to accommodate note-taking difficulties.

9. Getting down homework assignments quickly and correctly can be a difficult task for the child with a handwriting disability. Ask your child's teacher to consider ways to make this task easier.

   Writing down assignments at the end of the period or day is not realistic. Many teachers put the assignments on the board in the morning, and they remain there all day. The student has ample opportunity to copy them down throughout the day without being rushed.

   The teacher may want to write in the assignment for the child or check for assignment accuracy and completeness and initial the plan book each day. This courtesy helps the child and alerts the parents to what is to be completed for homework.

   Many teachers follow the example of their college professors. When completing their lesson plans for the week, they make out an assignment sheet for each of their students. This idea not only alleviates the pressure of writing the assignment but also keeps the child who is absent from falling behind.

10. At home, becoming your child's "secretary" can be very helpful. Write down your child's ideas and thoughts so they can be preserved without the writing process interfering with your child's creativity. A tape recorder will accomplish the same goal.

11. Help your child approach writing assignments in a systematic way. These steps need to be completed over time.

    Begin by brainstorming all the thoughts and ideas he might want included in his paper. This is where your role as secretary will be helpful.

    After the brainstorming session comes the selection of those ideas which should be included in the paper. Sequencing of ideas in a logical manner is important. (An outline may be useful in this organizational step.) Next comes the writing of the rough draft. Again, you may want to write as he dictates or he may want to enter his thoughts directly into the computer.

The refinement of the work follows the rough draft. This is where spelling (spell check is a technological blessing!), grammar, and punctuation are corrected and thoughts are clarified or expanded. (Our recommendation is to do one part of the refinement process at a time so as not to get overwhelmed.)

Finally, the finished copy is ready to prepare.

12. Allow your child to use the method of writing easiest and most efficient for him. Some children, like Christian, prefer manuscript (printing). The simple circle-and-line formation of letters is much easier to learn and control. Other children find the flow of cursive (script) much more productive. While the production of cursive letters is much more difficult than manuscript, the pencil does not need to leave the paper as often, giving a much more consistent flow to the writing process. If by fourth or fifth grade your child is still having difficulty mastering cursive writing, it is best to move past this as an issue and allow him to choose which method to use.

13. A dialogue journal is an effective way of communicating with your child and reinforcing writing skills at the same time. This is conversation on paper. You write a message to your child and she writes a message back. A spiral notebook or a blank book will keep your messages intact. Some families communicate on the computer. Any topic may be written in the journal.

    Many busy moms and dads find this a nice way to keep in touch with their children. Darlene's children would make evening entries and she would respond when she arrived home after a late evening class. In the morning, her children would eagerly read their personal message from Mom. Everyone benefited because they all had an opportunity to communicate with each other every day.

Rules for using dialogue journals are simple:

• Accept anything your child writes. Your child is taking a risk by writing to you. If you are open and accepting of what your child is sharing, you may be amazed at the quality and quantity of the information you receive.

- Relax and enjoy. This should not become a mandatory, demanding activity. This is a time when you can sit back and get to know your child. It should be a pleasurable and nonthreatening experience for you and your child.

Communicating with Your Child's School

Parent-teacher conferences

The parent-teacher conference can occur for several reasons. The most common type of conference is the regularly scheduled meeting to discuss the child's progress in school. Most schools set aside one or two days a year for parents to come to school and discuss the academic progress of their child. These conferences usually occur after report cards have been sent home to parents. Parents are given a limited amount of time to meet with teachers and discuss in person what the report card has already stated.

At other times, parents and teachers may consult informally if academic, social, or behavioral concerns arise. These conferences may be called by either party, and usually a specific concern is discussed. If each respects the position of the other and there is a desire to work as partners to improve the situation, solutions emerge. Parents need to prepare for the conferences and learn to present themselves assertively.

Gateways to effective home-school communication

If frustration and desperation have peaked by the time a conference is scheduled, often tempers are ready to explode. Keeping in mind some of these pointers may defuse the situation and result in a more productive session.

1. Selection of the location for the meeting is very important. Resist the temptation to "catch" the teacher in a public place. The hallway, the school office, or an open classroom are not appropriate locations for a meeting. Arrange to meet your child's teacher in a private, confidential place out of the mainstream. After all, other adults and children do not need to overhear conversations concerning your child.

2. Come prepared with notes. Your questions and concerns should be written down so you can address every issue. Bring work samples, grades, or anything else that might be helpful. If you requested the conference, prepare an agenda of issues you want addressed. This preparation will help you keep the focus on your concerns.

3. Set the tone of the meeting to indicate your desire for collaboration and partnership, e.g. "I have some concerns about Mary I was hoping we could discuss and maybe together come up with ideas we could use to help her succeed." This is a much more effective approach than finger-pointing and demanding. Teachers are an important part of your support system. Asking "What can *we* do?" instead of "What are *you* going to do?" is much more productive.

4. An open, accepting posture is more conducive to opening the flow of communication than one closed and defensive. Finger-pointing or blaming will cause communication to break down and a hostile, nonproductive atmosphere to develop.

5. Allow enough time to adequately discuss your concerns and find solutions. Be sensitive to the demanding schedules teachers must follow. When scheduling a conference, offer several dates and times from which the teacher might choose. This courtesy allows them to adequately plan for the meeting.

6. Overuse of "teacher talk" (jargon) will cause parents to feel inferior and uncomfortable. For that reason, in this chapter and in the glossary we have introduced some of the terms you may hear at school meetings. Whenever a term is used you do not understand, ask for a definition.

Information on conferencing with your child's teachers to this point has been focused on how to interact effectively when a problem occurs. It also needs to be mentioned that giving positive feedback to your school is equally important. As humans, we seldom remember to pat each other on the back once in a while and say, "Good job!" When was the last time you were stopped by a police officer and congratulated on your fine driving ability? When was the last time you thanked someone for no specific reason?

The same applies in our interaction with the school. For some reason, parents and teachers feel that the only communication between them should be in time of crisis or to relate negative information.

Having been on both sides of the fence, we, the authors, can attest to the importance of positive feedback. As parents of children with ADD, we know only too well the intensity and anxiety of hearing that teacher's voice on the other end of the phone, *again!* There were times when the telephone became our worst enemy. The stress caused by those phone calls would then cause us to confront our sons, and that in turn would cause more stress. We felt threatened as parents and felt we were not doing a very good job. The constant string of telephone calls kept reinforcing this feeling.

This negative cycle would continue until someone would say or do something to remind us our children did have their positive side too. No one can boost a parent's self-esteem like a teacher who calls to share something positive once in a while.

However, be prepared. You will still tense up at hearing that familiar voice on the other end of the phone. We have become conditioned to hear the worst. Nancy recalls a time when Christian's principal, knowing her telephone anxiety, used to preface his conversations with her by saying immediately, "I'm not calling about Christian."

From the educator's perspective, a note of thanks or a gesture of appreciation for the support given to your child creates tremendous goodwill. Students with ADD can be very overwhelming within a classroom. Teachers often have five or more of these students at one time. (Think about this as you try to manage your one or two.) A note of appreciation when the teacher spends extra time with your child or implements strategies or interventions that help make school more manageable can be just the incentive needed to make the extra effort worthwhile. Too often parents jump in making demands but never return to say thank you when teachers meet the demands.

Nancy often shares a personal story illustrating the importance of positive feedback for both the parent and the teacher. Christian's sophomore year in high school was extremely difficult. His impulsivity was at an all-time high. During that year, he finally got himself suspended from school. During that stressful time, Nancy had to meet with his English teacher, Cathy Ransenberg. Without realizing it, Mrs. Ransenberg said exactly what Nancy needed to hear at that time to save her from feeling like a total failure as a parent. She related to Nancy that she and Christian's other teachers were sorry he was suspended but felt he was a good kid going through a difficult time and would be all right in the end. This teacher saw the potential in Christian's writing abilities and worked with him to develop his skills. She also was the drama teacher and got Christian involved in the school's productions, which turned out to be a positive release for him. These were two powerful influences in his life and affected his pursuit of a career in communications.

Upon Christian's graduation from high school, Nancy attempted to write in a note to Cathy Ransenberg how much those few words of support had meant to her at that difficult time in her life. To this day, Nancy still does not think that this teacher is fully aware of what she did for her. Every time Christian has seen this teacher in the past four years, she has always commented on Nancy's note of thanks and how much it meant to receive it, and remarked that she still has it.

Positive communication—a powerful motivator!

Home-school notes

Home-school notes are designed to provide frequent information for the parents. This is a very effective way to keep communication flowing with your child's teacher. This gives parents a way to provide constant guidance to the child as he learns to manage ADD.

The child with ADD might do well one week and totally fall apart the next. By the time midterm reports or end-of-the-quarter grades go home, the child who was passing at the last communication may be failing. Therefore, it is extremely important to closely monitor the progress of your child daily or at least on a weekly basis.

The home-school notes serve a dual purpose. First, parents receive information about behaviors, progress, long-term assignments, upcoming tests, incomplete assignments, and accomplishments. Second, teachers hear from the parents when there is a change within the family that could affect the child's functioning in school. Changes that might adversely affect a child include the separation or divorce of the parents, the birth of a sibling, a change in living arrangements, an accident, an illness, and a death in the family.

Teachers need to communicate to the parents changes, positive or negative, which they observe as a result of the child's medication. It is also important that parents be informed of the progress of any aspect of the management plan put in place for the child.

The benefits of the home-school notes are numerous. The greatest advantage is that the parents and teachers become partners when the goals have been defined and both are working together to achieve them. The left hand knows what the right hand is doing because the lines of communication are open and flowing on a regular basis. Parents, teachers, and the child all stay informed.

When setting up home-school notes with your child's teacher, the following points should be considered.

1. Identify areas interfering with your child's progress. Target specific concerns.
2. Prioritize. Select no more than three specific concerns to monitor and evaluate at one time. For example, if your child has a problem with missing assignments, then that may be your number-one priority.
3. Set small, realistic goals. For example, it may be more realistic in the beginning to expect your child to turn in homework three out of five days rather than all five. Then once he has suc-

cessfully reached this goal, gradually add the other two days. Goals that are unrealistic or too long-term defeat the purpose. If your child will earn an incentive on Friday for turning in all his homework each day and misses Tuesday's assignment, why should he keep up for the rest of the week? He already missed his goal.

4. Decide how often you will need to communicate. Once a day or once a week would be beneficial. We usually recommend monitoring be done daily in the beginning just to establish the structure and routine for everyone involved. Once improvement is observed, pull back to a weekly communication.

5. Select or design a quick and efficient note that is for the teacher to use, yet informative for you and your child. Plan books or daily planners can be a natural vehicle for daily communication. There are materials you can purchase designed for this purpose. Check your local school-supply stores.

   Design your own plan book. Include the child's name, teacher's name, date, specific goals you are trying to attain (incomplete assignments), a key to how you will evaluate (smiley faces, check marks, etc.), a space for each day of the week to be recorded, and a place for comments (see Figure 4-2).

   Many schools provide their own communication forms. Christian's high school had a report form available in the office each Friday. He took the Friday report around to all of his teachers for their comments and signatures.

6. Arrange with the teacher how and when that communication will arrive home.

7. Discuss who is responsible for what. Experience shows that when the home accepts the responsibility for the incentives and consequences, this becomes a more effective intervention. Teachers should provide and complete the note. For older students, it should become the child's responsibility to get the teacher to complete and sign the note once the system is in place.

8. Explain to your child the purpose of the notes and how the sys-

Figure 4–2
Home-School Communication

CHILD'S NAME:			DATE:		
TEACHER'S NAME:					
Goals	MON.	TUE.	WED.	THUR.	FRI.
1. Assignments turned in					
2. In class on time					
3. Asked questions on topic					

Comments:

key: I = Improvement seen
      N = No improvement

tem will work. Also help your child to understand his or her responsibility.

9. Together with your child, determine the incentives for appropriate and improved behavior. Incentives may be given immediately or your child may choose to work toward short-term goals. Incentives should be given within a week.

   Giving feedback on a daily basis in the beginning may be most effective. "If Mrs. Smith receives all your assignments tomorrow, you may ask a friend over to play for an hour after school." This goal appears attainable to the child.

   Extend the time to two or three days of completed assignments as you begin to see improvement. Gradually work toward weekly goals.

10. Consequences also need to be established if the child does not follow through with his responsibilities. Children with ADD become experts at bypassing the system. Christian had a thousand and one excuses when he did not have his Friday report.

Therefore, we established the rule "No Friday report, no football games" or other social activities over the weekend. For a teenager, a weekend with parents is the kiss of death. We consistently began to get Friday reports. However, missing assignments still prevailed. To address this, we asked the teachers to indicate which assignments were missing. We then established the rule that if he played all week and did not do his assignments, he had to do them over the weekend. After several weekends of playing catch-up, we began to see fewer missed assignments.

As with all suggestions and strategies there is always another side and another way of handling these communciations. Some schools provide this service through the school counselor or a special education teacher. Darlene's son Tom is enrolled in a tutorial program at his high school. Each Friday the tutorial instructor sends a progress note to parents. Each classroom teacher reports to the tutorial instructor on the past week's progress and advises of upcoming assignments. This enables the teacher to assist the students in planning and implementing strategies or interventions that may be necessary to successfully complete each assignment.

Who gathers the information is not nearly as important as assuring that communication takes place and strengthens the school/student/parent relationship.

Intervention assistance teams (IATs) or large school conferences

The purpose of an IAT meeting is usually to address more serious concerns that the school, or sometimes the home, is experiencing. These are usually issues teachers and parents have tried to resolve without success. Among these situations could be academic failure, suspension, or serious behavior problems. An IAT meeting usually involves many school personnel and the parents.

Even the most skilled speaker may find herself fumbling for words or being intimidated when sitting across the table from her child's teachers, principal, and other school personnel. This can be a very humbling and sometimes humiliating experience.

It is very difficult for a parent to hear anything negative about her child. The parent may be dealing simultaneously with a recent diagnosis of ADD and school problems stemming from the disorder. It may seem that the whole world is crashing down around her and that her child does nothing right. At this point, many parents, especially dads, go into a protective mode of denial. This is unproductive and only delays the inevitable. The troublesome situations must be met head on by finding workable solutions. Attending school meetings with advanced preparation can be a very good line of defense.

As a learning specialist, Nancy is the liaison between the school and the home. She tries to balance the two factions. It is her responsibility to find ways for the home and school to work collaboratively and form a partnership to support each other and the child involved.

However, when she needs to advocate for her own son, Christian, she often experiences the anxiety and frustration felt by the majority of parents. Because she is the emotional parent, her husband, David, always accompanies her to meetings concerning their son. David's presence accomplishes two goals. First, he is the voice of reason. He can calmly and rationally listen to what is being said and respond with his head, not his heart. Second, because of the emotional anxiety Nancy usually experiences in these meetings, she relies on David to explain and clarify for her afterward what was discussed and the outcome of the meeting. From that point, she can proceed to the resolutions or modifications Christian needs to resolve the problem.

The point of this anecdote is that no matter how qualified or prepared you feel, when it comes to your own child, your emotions tend to run higher and you may forget everything you wanted to say unless you have someone to support you. In Nancy's case, she and her husband work as an effective team. If you need support when attending school meetings, take a spouse, a friend, a relative, or your child's physician. The person you ask to attend with you may want to take notes, help you make a point, or help keep you focused on the points you wanted to make.

Another consideration in preparing for school conferences is to know your child's rights and how those rights are protected under the law. It is your right to be a part of the process when an IEP or 504 plan is being written for your child. The school needs to communicate and work with you as a partner in the goal-setting and accommodations that these two documents provide. You know better than anyone what your child needs to succeed. Therefore, your involvement in the process is very important in getting appropriate and effective support for your child. Signing a plan already completed may not be in your child's best interest. You may want to ask for revisions to be made. What parents have to say is important, and you deserve to be heard and included in decisions being made about your child's education.

Before attending any scheduled meeting, sit down and prioritize those things you hope to discuss. Be prepared to be flexible and ready to negotiate. At the top of your list, write the most important points on which you will not compromise. Follow with the negotiable items. Take this list with you to the meeting.

Try to enter the meeting with an open mind, ready to listen to the information being presented by the school. Even though you may be angry or frustrated or feel intimidated, being on the defensive will interfere with successfully getting your child's needs met.

During the meeting, keep in mind that *how* you communicate your thoughts and feelings can make more of a difference than *what* you say. Communicate your position assertively.

1. Look the participants in the eye. Avoid looking away or down. People take advantage of a passive communicator.
2. Use "I" statements to express your feelings and wishes. Finger pointing is unproductive and alienates others. Once this occurs, communication shuts down.
3. Follow the three Cs: State your position calmly, clearly, and concisely. Listen carefully to what others have to say and weigh the value of their opinions in your decision-making process.

4. Ask for clarification if you do not understand something. Teachers, using jargon all day, often forget that parents are not familiar with all the terms and phrases being used. Asking for explanations if this occurs helps you better understand what is being said about your child. Ask school personnel to use layman's terms in school meetings when teacher talk occurs.

5. Monitor your nonverbal behavior. Are your arms crossed defiantly in front of you? Are you leaning back in your chair as an observer or forward at the table as an active participant? Consider that in a conversation between two people, the words used convey less than 35 percent of the message while the nonverbal signals convey 55 percent. This is why mixed messages can be so confusing. When the mouth is saying something different from what the body is expressing, the body is the more powerful communicator.

6. All school conferences are considered confidential. If this is not mentioned in the beginning, it would be wise to have that point established.

7. At intervention-assistance team meetings, some record keeping is essential to document for future reference the concerns and responsibilities of the participants of the meeting, as well as the interventions used and the progress made. You may want to ask for a copy of these minutes for your records.

Communicating with your child's school can be a very powerful experience if you are all willing to work together as partners in the process. For both teachers and parents, finding the combinations to work successfully for the child is an exercise in effective problem solving. Each needs to respect and listen to the other's opinions if effective solutions are to be found. The next section will address the problem-solving process.

5

Problem Solving

Problem solving is about change. If a situation doesn't need changing, it is not a problem. Having a system or model to help navigate through or around problems gives us a way to direct our energy. Change doesn't come easily or quickly, but following the models below will help you develop the problem-solving skills you need. Remember, as you learn a new skill, pass it along by teaching your child. Effective problem solving is a collaborative effort. Be sure your child is part of the process.

Problems are part of life. Most can be easily resolved; others require more thought. How problems are approached varies from one person to another, but most of us follow some sequential method when problem solving. We would like to present a scenario you may recognize, and then proceed through the problem-solving process.

Mary, a usually agreeable child, turns into a screaming terror each evening at bedtime. She throws a tantrum when asked to turn off the TV and put away her toys. Her body goes limp and becomes dead weight when Dad tries to physically remove her. She scratches

and kicks if Mom tries to help. Getting her into the bathtub and prepared for bed is an additional battle. By the time Mary's parents finally get her into bed, everyone is worn out and angry. Closing the
door behind them is not the end of the story. Mary frequently leaves
her room, offering one excuse after another. Not until her parents
scream and threaten does Mary finally settle down and go to sleep.

The following model may help us resolve this difficult situation.

1. Identify and define the problem. This should be done in specific
   terms. Describe the symptoms or characteristics you observe.
   All concerns related to this problem also should be identified.
   In our example, the problem is identified as getting Mary to go
   to bed and stay there without the evening struggle. The problem is further defined as the chaos and disharmony within the
   family caused by Mary's tantrums. She is demonstrating inappropriate behavior by screaming, kicking, and fighting her parents. Her lack of cooperation is making evenings intolerable.

2. Analyze the problem. Examine all possible causes of the problem. Write down all ideas, no matter how wild or bizarre they
   seem. In our example, there may be several factors causing
   Mary's behavior.

   Mary is quite happy doing what she wants to do. She does
   not want to be disturbed and leave the center of activity. She
   may not want her day to end. She may have problems when
   she is abruptly asked to stop one activity and begin another.
   She may be lonely in her room. These may all be logical explanations for Mary's behavior.

3. Brainstorm solutions. Again, list any ideas that come to mind.
   Do not stifle your creativity! In our scenario, using a timer to
   give Mary advanced notice that bedtime is approaching might
   be a solution. Have Mary pick up her toys before the TV is
   turned on. Limit the viewing of TV to one or two shows per
   evening. Have Mary prepare for bed before she is allowed to
   watch TV. Give Mary something to look forward to once she is
   ready for bed—a story, a song, quiet time with Mom or Dad.

Make it clear that Mary is to stay in her room once the door is closed. Give her the option of reading or listening to music until she is ready to go to sleep.

4. Make a plan of action. Select strategies to implement. Explain to Mary she will receive a fifteen-minute warning when TV time is ending. She will be expected to turn off the TV when the bell sounds. If she complies, she may select a story to be read when she is bathed, brushed, and in bed within twenty minutes (or whatever is a reasonable time) after the TV has been turned off. If she does not comply, then no TV the next evening.

5. Evaluate the results of your efforts. Was giving Mary advanced notice of change helpful? Was having something to look forward to effective? Were there observable changes in Mary's behavior?

6. Implement additional strategies until you resolve the problem. Continue to select from the ideas you brainstorm until a workable combination is found to get Mary to cooperate and peaceably go to bed. If Mary is now going to bed without a tantrum but still leaves her room, then find ways to resolve that part of the problem.

7. Go back to the beginning of the process if the problem reappears. If your plan of action works for a while but then the behavior begins to resurface, go back and redefine and identify the breakdown, analyze why the problem recurred, brainstorm solutions, make a plan of action, implement the strategies, and evaluate.

Intervention Assistance Teams

This problem-solving process may now be implemented in your child's school. Many states are now requiring school districts to develop and implement an intervention assistance team for each school in the district. (Different states call this collaborative problem-solving process by different names, but they all have similar designs and serve the same purpose.) An intervention assistance team, or IAT, addresses the needs of the child and provides the classroom teacher, support personnel, and parents with concrete ways to help the child learn and succeed.

Each IAT will have the same major components but will vary in some respects to meet the needs of each individual school. Each model should have a core team, or standing committee, consisting of the same participants that attend every IAT meeting. Depending on the support personnel available to each school, the core team usually includes the principal, classroom teacher, special education teacher, school psychologist and/or school counselor, and the parents of the child.

An auxiliary team, or ad hoc committee, may also be added. This team usually includes additional personnel who may provide services to the child referred or additional insight on the problem presented. Members of the auxiliary team may include the school nurse, a tutor, the speech and language pathologist, a former teacher, a social worker, or resources from the community such as clergy, physicians, or drug and alcohol counselors.

As mentioned, the IAT is designed to be a collaborative problem-solving body. The purpose is *not* to place blame. It is *not* to attack parents or school personnel. An IAT meeting is an opportunity for parents and professionals to sit down together, identify the problem, brainstorm solutions, design a plan of action to attempt to resolve the problem, and support each other in the process. An IAT should definitely be a part of the parents' support system.

How does an IAT work? The process is begun with a teacher's referral of the child to the team. Before the referral is made, the teacher should have consulted with the parents and other school personnel about the concerns the child is presenting. When all attempts to resolve the problem have been exhausted, the teacher presents the child's name before the IAT. At this time, the facilitator, or leader of the team—usually the principal—calls together the core team and any auxiliary personnel who could contribute to the process. It is important to mention at this point that anyone can request an IAT meeting including the parents. However, it is usually the classroom teacher who makes the referral.

How does an IAT meeting work? How frequently IAT meetings are held depends upon the school. Some meet every day and others are held once or twice a month. The meetings follow the problem-solving model designed by the school. Each school varies, but usually the following steps appear somewhere in the agenda.

1. Meetings usually begin with the teacher describing the problem and what interventions she has tried on her own.
2. Once the problem has been clearly identified and defined, possible reasons for the problem are offered.
3. Then begins the brainstorming process. Everyone present offers ideas to bring resolution to the problem. These ideas are recorded by the IAT record keeper.
4. Then an intervention plan is formulated. Suggestions from the brainstorming are examined and some are selected for implementation. Various members of the team assume responsibility for carrying them out. For example, allowing the child to take tests untimed and out of class may be a suggestion. The resource teacher or tutor may volunteer to make the time and place available for the student.
6. Once the plan has been completed and everyone understands how the plan will be supported, a time is scheduled to meet and evaluate the results of the action taken. A two- to three-week period is average.

If the concept of an Intervention Assistance Plan is new to you, we strongly urge you to contact the principal of your child's school or the school district superintendent or your state board of education. One final thought: the mandate for an IAT is to include the parents as collaborative partner in their child's education. However, it is amazing how many schools have IATs that do not have parents as a member of the core team. It is your right and obligation to take an active role in the decision-making process in matters concerning your child's welfare and education. Do not feel intimidated and do not be excluded. Only you can be your child's best advocate in getting his or her needs met.

Down-and-Dirty Conflict Resolution

Once you understand how to use the problem-solving model, there is no end to the possible applications of this skill. Opportunities present themselves daily, especially in the family.

It is no longer the norm for Dad to work while Mom stays home. Parents share responsibilities for outside work and family. We are not devaluing Dad's role here. Regardless of the changes in family structure or responsibility, many more mothers seem to inherit the role of mediator. Is that why mediator starts with an *m?* Mothers have been mediating problems forever, separating siblings and running interference between neighborhood children and their own. The fun just never ends.

Whoever is the mediator in your home can use the three-step "down-and-dirty" model when tempers flare and intervention is needed.

Remember to use that FM voice and those "I" statements. You are the voice of reason. You are the one who interprets each point of view, and summarizes facts and feelings. Keep a cool head and a soft tone and the mediation will be more effective.

Step One: Defuse and define.

Conflict is like any other problem. Before you can address the problem, you have to define it. In heated exchanges, this may be difficult. Start by defusing the anger. Ask each child what he thinks is the problem. Only one child speaks at a time and must not interrupt when another is speaking. Summarize what he has said and how he feels about what happened. Then confirm your understanding by paraphrasing his statements and asking for agreement.

Step Two: What have you tried? What can you do?

Have the children attempted to resolve this? In what way? What happened when they tried? What can each child do right now? What can they do in the future to keep something like this from happening again? What happens if you do nothing? Brainstorm solutions to the above. Follow the rules of valuing each person's ideas and active listening.

Step Three: Resolution.

What solution does each child prefer? Is there any solution they can't agree to? Come to a solution each child can agree with. Summarize points of agreement. Show how each person's needs are being met by the decision. Is the agreement specific and balanced? Affirm and praise the contribution made by each child to the problem-solving process. State the agreement out loud. Get confirmation from each child that he agrees to it and have kids signal their agreement with a handshake or hand slap "five."

Let's suppose Oscar and Felix are our children and they share a room. You may know that Oscar is the world's biggest slob. Felix is a little on the fussy side. Each of our delightful children despises the other's method of cleaning. They have literally come to blows because you have sent them (two children with ADD) to their room to clean.

FELIX: You are a slob. I'm going to throw everything of yours out the window.

OSCAR: What's the big deal! Leave my stuff alone or I'm going to pop you. *(Oscar drops another creek-soaked sock on the hardwood floor.)*

FELIX: Leave those socks in here and I'll burn them.

Unless you love repeat performances or can afford to buy a new house and put the two boys in separate wings, this situation cries for mediation. It might work something like the following.

1. **Defuse and define:** Oscar might state he thinks Felix is too fussy and too bossy, and he is angry that he can't have his room as he wants it. He can't find anything when Felix cleans. Disorder may drive Felix to the edge. He can't stand the mess and can't function in chaos. He is overwhelmed and stressed by clutter. After each presents his side, restate each person's position, showing that you understand his point of view and feelings.

2. **What have you tried?** So far, fighting and throwing have been tried. Threats and name calling have also been used. This hasn't worked, because no one has changed the way he does things.

   What else can you try? Felix could burn the socks or throw all the clutter out the window. That might work. Probably not. It will more than likely escalate the problem.

   They could draw an imaginary line down the room and make each person responsible for his side. Of course they might just fight about whose side of the room the junk is on. The room could be divided by bookshelves so no one but Oscar can see the mess. Perhaps Felix can agree to tolerate a certain amount of clutter.

3. **Resolution.** In this scenario, it is impossible to completely satisfy either party. The best solution is a compromise. Oscar agrees not to block access to Felix's dresser, the closet, or the bedroom door. He also agrees to keep a certain amount of clutter out of sight. This means shoving it under the bed, but Felix will tolerate any clutter he doesn't see. If Oscar forgets and leaves his mess in the road, Felix has permission to dump it all in the middle of his bed.

   They still aren't in love, but they have agreed on tolerance. There will still be times when these two opposites clash. But the more you mediate and model problem-solving behavior, the easier it will be to resolve conflicts that arise.

Back to time-out

There will be times when emotions are too heated to resolve the problem. It is then appropriate to take time out and let emotions cool. In the home, children can be separated and brought back together. For parent-child conflict, it may be appropriate to let everyone sleep on the situation. Parents can't effectively mediate when they are emotionally charged. "We're all too upset to solve this now," you might say. "Let's make an appointment tomorrow morning after breakfast for a family meeting."

If the conflict involves a neighbor's child, ask the children to sit ten feet apart. Explain the idea of resolving conflict and let each know you value them and their feelings and want to see them find an answer to the problem.

Ask each child to agree to work out the problem and follow the down-and-dirty method. Ideally, parents would love to resolve every conflict when it happens. The reality is, there is a chance you might not get past the defuse-and-define stage in the beginning. That's OK. You've planted a seed and given the kids something to think about.

Parents don't need to intervene in every scrabble in which their child is involved. Often kids will have an argument and forget about it within five minutes. Most parents can sense when intervention is necessary. If someone can be hurt—if rocks or sticks are involved, for instance—immediate intervention is necessary. If a child is being shamed or being made the scapegoat in a situation, intervention may be necessary.

Words can hurt

"Sticks and stones may break my bones, but words will never hurt me." This delightful little ditty has probably passed the lips of everyone who ever was a child. Most of us recognize it for what it is: a crock of cow patties. Words do hurt.

This may not seem to be a problem, but it can be. If your child initiates or is the receiver of hurting words, it is useful to intervene.

We do not mean simply informing the offender that his behavior is "not nice." We recommend intervention by raising awareness.

Children are made fun of for their body shape, teeth, hair, skin color, and learning or physical differences. This should not be tolerated. All children need an awareness and appreciation of differences. Children with ADD can be unintentionally cruel. They speak without thinking. They may tell a friend his favorite possession is ugly, his dog is stupid, and his hair is weird and then be surprised by the negative response. They are often on the receiving end of criticism.

The goal for solving this problem is to decrease the number of put-downs based on differences. Help children become aware and appreciate each person's uniqueness. Informal games or conversations about favorite smells, foods, songs, colors, or places help children find commonalities. Finding differences can be an opportunity to experience something new. Did a neighbor's child live in a different place? Can your child do something unusual, such as juggling? Sharing these experiences help children develop pride in their individuality and respect for the differences in others.

Setting Goals

Another application of the problem-solving model is in defining and setting goals. Goals can be small or large, short- or long-term. Goals can apply to scholastic, social, or personal achievement. Setting goals and reaching them can be a never-ending challenge for children with ADD.

Inattention or distractibility may make it difficult to stick with any goal for long. The longer it takes to reach a goal, the more likely children with ADD will become sidetracked.

The following goal-setting model can be found in the book *Esteem Builders,* by Dr. Michele Borda. This book has an excellent section on step-by-step goal setting, overcoming obstacles, and results analysis. Have your child pick a goal and set up a step-by-step plan for reaching it.

By now you are probably sick of hearing it. Start, as always, by defining your goal. What do you want to be better at? What do you want to learn? Suppose you want to play the guitar.

Plan how you will accomplish this. What things do you need? Who will you need to help you? When will you start? The first goal might be getting a guitar. If you have a guitar, perhaps you need to take lessons. Perhaps you need a study strategy.

Let's suppose you have a guitar and are taking lessons. How can you improve your skills? Who can help you? Talk with your instructor or someone you admire and ask how he might reach this goal. The instructor may suggest doing scales or chords for fifteen minutes every Monday, Wednesday, and Friday. Tuesday and Thursday, you practice songs. Decide when in each day you will do this. Pick a song you would like to play better (a smaller goal). How long should it take to achieve this if you follow your plan?

Measure. How close are you to that goal now? Do you know most of the chords, the beat, or notes? How far do you need to go until you reach it? Do you need to learn bar chords or power chords to play this song? Do you know how to pick? Does it matter? Is the song more difficult than you thought? Will it take longer? Can you reach it faster?

Write a goal statement saying what you plan to achieve. Draw a picture of yourself achieving that goal.

Decide when you want to achieve the goal. Do you want to play your song for a recital. For a friend's birthday?

Accentuate the positive. Visualize yourself meeting the goal. Each week, as you keep your practice schedule, praise yourself for keeping on target. Track how close you are to your goal and when you will achieve it. Have you learned three of five new chords? Do you need to switch finger positions more quickly? How is the plan coming?

Finally, evaluate your success. Are you happy with the results? If so, congratulate yourself and thank those who helped you. If not, decide what were the obstacles and what you can do differently.

Our final approach to problem solving deals with changing your community. Communities can represent your neighborhood, school building, school district, or entire city.

Facilitating Change in Your Community

If we want to see positive changes in our school communities, we need to understand how change happens and what we, as parents, can do to facilitate it. Warren G. Bennis, Ph.D., and former president of the University of Cincinnati, developed the following three general strategies that effect change. Understanding how change happens helps us develop a frame of reference and a plan or problem-solving strategy for becoming change agents.

The first is the empirical-rational strategy. This strategy assumes that people will adopt proposed changes if they can be rationally justified through research, analysis, and clarification. We can use this strategy to facilitate change at the classroom level and schoolwide.

Begin by gathering sound information about ADD or your child's specific learning problem into your personal resource file. You can do this by attending workshops and reading books or journals. Copy relevant articles and highlight particularly relevant information. Never rely on just one source or piece of information to support or explain your point. Find several sources that discuss the same issue, if possible, from different approaches. Use the bibliographies in interesting articles to broaden your knowledge base. Become familiar with the library in your community or a nearby college. Learn how to use its computer system to do literature searches. Most libraries have assistants who will guide you through this process. Gather this information and assemble your evidence before you approach the teacher or school administration.

Do not let this process intimidate you. It does take time, but it is not difficult. Two of the most successful parent advocates we know had no more than a high-school education and a burning desire to help their children. They were motivated by a crisis in their children's lives and the unwillingness or inability of their school to provide the support their children needed.

Use the guidelines in the communications section on parent-school conferences to prepare your case and plan your approach or intervention strategy. Do not approach your school with an "I want" strategy. Clarify the problem and then propose possible interventions supported by the expert testimony gathered in your resource book.

There are times when schools might not be receptive to your suggestions. Don't become discouraged. Think of these initial sessions as cultivating the soil and planting the seeds of change. Step back and give change some time.

We did not walk into our schools with a big stick, demanding change. We walked in with data, expert testimony, and options. We walked in again and again and again. Darlene jokes that the reason her children's school was so helpful with modifications is they just got sick of her and would do anything to get rid of her.

In reality, most schools treasure the parents who care about their children and their work and achievement. The key in addressing these issues is preparation and a professional approach, stressing partnership.

The second strategy that may effect change is the normative-reeducation strategy. This strategy assumes that change will occur only as the people involved revise what is for them a normal pattern of thinking. As we indicated earlier in this book, federal mandates require states to provide services for children with handicaps, including ADD. But years ago, the norm was for children with many disabilities to be turned away from school. There was no room in the inn for children needing modifications in the curriculum or environment. Today schools are required to provide for these children. They can no longer say there's no room, we don't have a program, or we don't have the money to provide these services. That is the new norm.

As school districts follow these mandates, they may change the way they think about and act toward children with disabilities. They may discover providing these services and serving this population enhances their school and learning for all children. They will have become reeducated.

The third strategy for effecting change is the power-coercive strategy. This strategy assumes you can implement change most effectively through political or economic sanctions. This can be done by parents through state regulatory agencies, or by filing a lawsuit. Another option is due process—the legal process for the educational system. When two parties disagree on recommendations or assessments and the conflict cannot be resolved by mediation, a due process hearing may be requested by either party.

We know of parents who have successfully been involved in due process with their child's school. This is a long, drawn-out process. The process is designed to be a safety net for children, but depending on how old your child is, he could have graduated or dropped out before you resolve everything. Even when courts or hearing officers rule in favor of the parents and mandate specific strategies or services, the school may drag its feet on implementing them.

We are not saying change can't happen this way. It can. Federal laws benefiting children with ADD would not be in existence otherwise. The question is, Do you have the energy and the resources to go this route?

You also have to decide whether it is worth putting yourself in an adversarial position with school authorities. Once this path is taken, you may never be able to repair relations with your school. Obviously, if this strategy is the only way to get the support and intervention necessary to ensure your child's survival in the academic world, the relationship with the school may take second place. We recommend this only as a last resort.

Five-Step Approach to Community Planning and Problem Solving

About now, you might wonder why in the world a book on parenting children with ADD would have a section on community planning and problem solving. Sometimes we need to motivate our schools or the larger community to change before our children get needed services or interventions. Problem solving is about bringing about these changes. The five-step process is about putting the plan together. You have been exposed to several problem-solving models. The first step in this model is different from the previous models. This prepares the way for implementation of problem solving at the community level. This model was presented by Art Knighton, a professor in the School of Social Work at the University of Cincinnati. We have modified the model somewhat to fit our purposes, but the basic steps are the same. This model illustrates how you can change your community. We will use the Attention Deficit Disorders Council of Greater Cincinnati (ADDC) to illustrate the model.

As parents, you may feel powerless to change your school, let alone the community at large. Believe us when we say this can be done.

Step One: Gearing up.

If you are the only one who sees a problem, you will not get much support in devising interventions. Gearing up means getting the community in the right frame of mind. In order to accomplish this, you must know your community.

What drives your community? What do its people think, feel, and want? Do they value conformity? Do they value each child as an individual? What are they concerned about? What are their expectations about children and education? Is your school district's response to problems expulsion or suspension? Are there support services in the schools or community for children with special needs?

Who are the leaders? In your school, this could be a psychologist, a counselor, or a learning disabilities teacher. In the larger community, it might be a group of physicians, an educational consultant, or a community organization. Can you enlist their support or gain insight into the community by networking with them?

Who are the stakeholders? Are there other parents who have children struggling with similar problems? How can you locate them? Two parents placed an ad in their local paper announcing a meeting for parents of children who were experiencing difficulty at school in their district. They expected a handful of parents to attend. They were flabbergasted when more than fifty parents showed up!

When the ADDC was started, we met in the hall of a building

owned by a local church. One evening a mother tentatively came into the hall. "Is this the meeting for parents of kids with ADD?" she asked. She was assured she was in the right place. "You mean all these people have kids with ADD? I thought I was at a bingo game." This mother thought she was all alone. It's a real comfort to discover just how many stakeholders there are in your community.

Become partners with your community by developing rapport and trust. This increases the chance that team building and sharing of resources will occur. Shared resources might be meeting spaces, professional advice, information, and volunteers.

Setting a mission is the final step in gearing up. What changes do we want, and why do we want them? The ADDC wants the community to understand the many aspects of living with ADD. We want that because when parents and school personnel are educated, they can make better choices for this population and improve the quality of life.

Step Two: Community assessment and analysis.

The purpose is to identify and target issues or conditions for change. This process is akin to doing a needs assessment. Determine the most pressing needs. What is the quality of current community resources? Where can children be tested? Are there any local support groups? How do organizations in your community interact? Do they share information and resources? Do schools have intervention teams? Do community members volunteer their time or expertise to serve on these teams? Form focus groups to determine what community members need and want. Hopefully the outcome of this analysis will be to develop a solution or design possible interventions.

Step Three: Develop solutions.

The ADDC discovered there were very few resources or educational materials available to parents or professionals in the community. Parents wanted links to community resources and information on educational, parenting, and behavioral interventions for their children. Educators wanted information regarding teaching strategies.

The solution was to develop a plan to provide this information to the general community.

Step Four: Implement the plan.

Set up your agenda and carry out the plan to deliver the intervention or program. The ADDC implemented a plan to deliver education to the community. A committee was formed to develop educational handbooks. Donations were obtained from a local veterans group to underwrite the initial printing cost. Handbooks were sold and some were donated to local schools and libraries.

Monthly educational meetings featuring local experts were organized, a newsletter was developed, and links to community resources were formed. Workshops featuring nationally known experts were organized and conducted.

Perhaps your plan would be to develop a school support group or provide in-service training for teachers. You might wish to discover which mental health professionals are experienced in treating ADD.

Step Five: Monitor and evaluate the solution.

This is often the most difficult and tiresome activity, especially for all-volunteer groups like the ADDC. So much energy and time goes into development and implementation that there is little enthusiasm left over for evaluation.

As tiresome as this step is, it is very necessary and does not need to be complicated. A basic method of record keeping can be followed. Record the number of people attending meetings, the number of educational materials sold, newsletters sent, and general-information requests filled.

Following this simple method, the ADDC can identify which parts of the tristate area are receiving their services and which out-of-state communities have received information from the group.

When the council organizes workshops, program evaluation is part of the process. Information is gathered on the quality of the program, the background of the attendees, and interest in future topics.

The council has no office and does not receive any grants to support its activities. Monitoring and evaluating the results of its actions is still important. Human resources are very limited; the group must carefully decide how to invest their personnel and other resources and which projects might provide the greatest benefit. Having this kind of data lets them monitor the success of programs and allocate resources in the most efficient way.

Models, Models, Models

We have given you several different models for solving problems. You have learned about problem solving in the home and in the school. You have been introduced to methods for helping you or your child establish and reach goals. You have a plan of action for influencing change in your school or community.

You will have many opportunities to practice these skills. Which model you use isn't as important as having a process you can rely on.

There is no more important skill for all children to carry into adulthood than the skill of cooperation and problem solving. Our families and neighborhoods are only small samples of the work, school, and social communities our children need in order to survive in this ever-evolving world.

Nothing is greater than having a plan come together, reaching a goal, or resolving a conflict. One potential roadblock is a lack of organizational skills. It is imperative to be able to organize information clearly enough to recognize options and where to get help, or to understand what the problem is. The models do provide a format to assist you in organizing information and developing a plan. Organization is not a natural gift for many people—just ask Darlene. If you or your child still find this difficult, the next chapter will be helpful. Remember there is no one way or right way to be organized.

6

Organization

Lack of organization is the bane of existence for many children with ADD. How your child's organizational difficulties are manifested or what kind of mind he has will dictate the types of possible interventions. How does your child approach a task? Is your child a global thinker? Does he need to know the outcome or the big picture before he can work on a task? Does he prefer taking tasks apart and doing them step by step? Does it depend on the task?

Organizational difficulties can make life a challenge, but don't beat yourself up if these are a problem for you. Learn what situations are problematic and then devise a solution that is the best for you and your way of working and understanding.

Difficulty with Organizing Materials

Ever heard the saying "Everything has a place and everything is in its place"? If your method of organization is closer to "Everything is someplace," you may have difficulty with material organization.

Individuals with this type of organizational problem may find it difficult to keep track of things. Children may constantly lose pencils, notebooks, and other tools needed to complete tasks. Parents might forget appointments or misplace their car keys or glasses.

The desk or locker may resemble a black hole into which books, homework, and reports fall, never to return. Under the bed may be a scary place inhabited by critters who eat socks or suck up Legos or Barbie's clothes.

Parents may see that homework is completed, check it again as their child walks into the school, only to have it magically disappear before class begins. Who knows where it went?

These problems are typical of the child with material organizational difficulties. Providing external structure or organization may benefit these children.

The best advice is to keep it simple. It is amazing that parents and professionals devise elaborate organizational processes and then wonder why the kids aren't able to get on board. Brainstorm with your child, keeping in mind his organizational difficulties and his strengths when designing interventions.

Pitfalls

Don't clean the room of a child who has material organizational difficulties without his assistance or permission. You are not doing him a favor and shouldn't be surprised when he yells, "Why did you touch my stuff? I can't find anything." These kids survive with a certain amount of clutter. When everything is in its place, they can't find anything! Learn to tolerate a certain level of disorder.

Another pitfall for children with material disorganization is having to do term papers with note cards. This is an organizational nightmare. Teachers love this method. Books have been written about it. For children or adults having difficulty with environmental organization, this is extremely stressful. There are too many papers, notes, cards, and props to organize and keep track of.

An alternative is to use a computer word-processing program to help you organize term papers. If this isn't available, keeping information for each source on a single sheet of notebook paper can be helpful. As you may recall, the note-cards method could require a dozen cards for a single source. Use a different color of paper for each source. When it is time to organize your term paper, paste your source sheets side by side on a long master sheet (use a roll of shelf or wrapping paper). Use a glue stick that isn't permanently adhering and you can move your information around until you get it in the right order. Since you have used a different color of paper for each source, you can see at a glance which sources you are using and how your information is organized.

Children who have strong visual or tactile skills may benefit from piecing the report together like a puzzle or developing it like a story board. If you use a long scroll of paper for the rough draft, they can see the report in its entirety. This benefits children who need to see the big picture, and although they may be handling several pieces of paper, they are not loose papers that can be dropped or misplaced.

This method may make many teachers shudder, and many parents will think it is the most outrageous thing they have ever heard of. If your method of organization is linear, step by step, you will hate it. If you have the ability to keep lots of materials together, you will most likely be successful with more traditional methods of organizing long-term assignments. But if an inability to keep track of lots of papers is keeping your child from completing long-term assignments, think about an alternative method of organization. We are not advocating using this method, and we use the word "method" loosely. This is just another example of how one person used his strengths and the knowledge of how he worked to organize his materials and space. Keep that in mind when you try to organize your child and his space or devise a strategy for long-term activities.

Color coding

Schools delight in and many children benefit from organization by color coding. Color coding helps children quickly locate all materials for a specific subject by assigning each subject a different color. All reading books, folders, and notebooks might be red. Math books and notebooks might be green. At the end of the school day, children check their planner or assignment notebook to determine in which subjects they have homework. If they have math homework, they bring home everything green. This is helpful for children who bring things home but not the right things. Some children use colored pens to write in their planners.

Color coding can be especially helpful for the disorganized child who must change classes. One quick look into the locker and you know which notebooks or books are needed for the upcoming class. Science coming up next? Grab blue.

A caution needs to be issued. Color coding books and folders will be helpful for some children. But if color coding means tripling the number of folders and notebooks, you may be asking for trouble.

Just do what comes naturally

Any organizational method is worth trying, but many will fail. When left to his own devices, a child may invent his own system. If it works, go with it.

Tim has terrible difficulties with material organization. He continually left books at school, couldn't find papers to turn in, and got in trouble for not doing homework. This was very frustrating as each night his parents would check his assignment notebook to be sure each assignment had been completed.

Tim's parents devised a plan that required them to initial his homework notebook beside each assignment as it was completed. If the teachers saw the initial, Tim was given until the end of the day to find the wayward homework. This often can be an effective bypass strategy, but for Tim it did not solve the problem.

Finally, Tim resolved the problem accidentally. He began sticking notebook papers in his book to mark the page of his homework assignment. This clutter of papers made his desk and books look a mess. But each afternoon he knew to put every book with a paper in it into his book bag. When the homework was completed it was placed back in the book. These visual reminders got the books and, more important, the homework back to class each day.

You would think he would lose papers from the book, but he never did. Instead of individual notebooks, one binder kept all long-term assignments or notes for every class. This did mean he often carried material he did not need with him all day. A small price to pay to ensure you have what you need when you need it.

Once again we are not recommending this method of organization. We are offering it as an illustration of how a child uses his creativity to discover what works for him or her.

Temporal-Sequential Organization

Children experiencing difficulties with temporal-sequential organization may appear very neat and organized. Instead of problems with materials, they experience difficulty with multiple-step tasks. They know where all their tools are but are unable to proceed through several steps in the correct order to get a task completed. Multistep math problems or spelling may be a difficulty.

Children may confuse time concepts such as before and after or how long a month is. This can make long-range planning a challenge, because tomorrow never comes. Then all of a sudden the day of the report has arrived and they can't explain why they haven't finished or even started it. Problems with remembering order of classes or lock combinations at the beginning of each school year may be seen. Difficulty in allotting time to tasks may result in tardiness.

Writing it down helps children with these difficulties. Tape schedules on their binders or planners. Get watches with alarms to get the kids home on time. Use timers to help break up tasks. A word of caution: Don't turn these strategies into pressure-filled situations where the clock becomes the enemy. Do what comes naturally and allow your child to use his strengths.

Sequencing difficulties may have a big impact on academics. Children may experience difficulty when writing reports. They may have difficulty deciding what should be the introductory sentence, what should be in the middle, or how to close. They may experience problems with breaking work into small tasks, deciding which should come first, or performing tasks in a logical order.

Wanted: Organizational Skills

All children and all adults need to be organized. The challenge is not just in organizing the external environment but also in devising a method or system of completing tasks. Children with ADD may need special training in organizational skills. They need assistance in bypassing organizational difficulties until they become competent. These skills are difficult to master, and much time and patience will be needed.

1. Teach children to summarize. Identify main ideas and develop scanning skills. Having textbooks where they can underline or write in the margins is advantageous. Help children learn to outline. Break some material into smaller sequential segments.
2. Help children learn to use assignment pads or long-term planners. Help children learn to break tasks into smaller segments and allocate enough time to complete them.
3. Keep calendars at home so children can keep track of activities. Parents may color code activities. All of Pam's activities or appointments are green; all of Joey's are purple. Kids can instantly look at the calendar and determine their schedule for the day. Schedule free or fun time to keep children from becoming overwhelmed. Have children note dates when projects are due or when items for the bake sale need to be turned in. This calendar helps not only the child but also the parents, who are often harried by their own lack of organization or by the responsibilities of parenting a child with ADD.
4. Help children learn the best time for them to study. Some chil-

dren need to rest after school and do homework after dinner. Other children may prefer to do homework immediately after school while it is fresh in their mind.

5. Help your child learn to use indexes and to identify pertinent information when researching reports or reading resource books. This helps the child who is not detail-oriented locate information.

Places and Spaces: How to Organize Them

Give your child a head start on homework by helping him set up his own work space. Find a well-lit place with minimal distractions. Have all tools handy. Some parents have used plastic washbasins to keep all study materials or supplies handy.

Be flexible about work spaces and places. Check your home for the most sensible space. Make sure the space is free of distractions. Remember, what is distracting for one person might not be for another.

Visual distractions may be a problem. Working near an open window or in view of the parakeet's or hamsters' cage may encourage dreams of safari. If your child's room is full of toys, they may distract him from completing homework or studying. A place away from distractions and near enough to the mainstream to allow supervision, monitoring, and availability is preferable.

Understand your child's learning style before you nix stereos or radios. These will be distracting for some children, but others find it difficult to concentrate without some background noise. Absolute quiet leads them to mental fatigue; halfway through the homework session, the child is falling asleep.

If your child has difficulty with time management, it may be necessary to establish some rules. Children who rush through homework may need a minimum time assigned. When homework assignments are finished in less than fifteen minutes, your child can have a small break and spend the remaining allotted time on review or study.

Often children with ADD don't think of reviewing and studying as homework. Plan time for these activities in each study session. Perhaps the first fifteen minutes can be spent reviewing, the next half hour can be spent on assignments, and the final fifteen minutes on more review or reading.

To Thine Own Self Be True

As authors and human beings, we approach organizational tasks from different perspectives. Neither way is right or wrong. The way that works best for each of us is the right way for that person. These differences made collaboration on this book a delight. Our strengths complemented each other and provided a balanced view of parenting a child with ADD.

Darlene's way

I belong to the "Everything is someplace" school of organization. I'm not ADD, but I still struggle with organizational difficulties. I believe this is in part because of the way I approach tasks. I work best with a global picture. I am not a detail person. This does not mean I don't understand or can't pay attention to details. This means details come at the end of the process for me. I like to understand the outcome and see the big picture before I approach a task. I like knowing why and how things happen but may struggle with details like names and dates. I can find my way home (big idea), but may not be able to find the book or bill when I need it (little idea).

Whether I am writing a book, a school paper, or a computer program, I need to see the big picture. When I have a program to do, I work best if I can visualize what should be the outcome. What is the goal of the report; what information should it contain? With that knowledge I will devise a plan to achieve the goal. If someone assigns a task and doesn't relate it to the big picture, it makes me crazy!

When writing this book, I approached the task by conceptualizing the message of the book, the important ideas I wanted to communicate. Then I sequentially organized the material in my mind before my fingers ever touched the keyboard.

My environment may be totally disorganized, but I have strong sequential-organization skills. In my mind, ideas seem to fall into place. Knowing where I want to be allows me to pick and choose information. I can think about what I need to know and where to get that information.

There are times when I must be detail-oriented or organize my materials. At these times, I rely on a self-imposed structure. This is not natural, but I can maintain it when necessary. The challenge arises when school quarters change or a project is finished. At these times of transition, I must change my organizational structure and adjust to a new one. Lucky for me I'm very flexible!

Backup and bypass

When I am in school, I use a planner. I keep one notebook or binder that contains a syllabus and notes for every class and a master planner at home. Every paper I write is saved on the hard drive and two floppy disks in addition to the paper copy I turn in. At work I have meeting reminders or deadlines tacked at eye level. These self-imposed tools keep me on track and prevent my organizational deficits from having a negative impact on my productivity.

My oldest son, Tim, and I share organizational styles. (We use the word "organizational" loosely.) When Tim brought home assignments for term papers that required note cards, I wanted to scream, and he wanted to quit. For us, using note cards is like playing fifty-two-card pickup. Note cards might make good book markers, but use them to organize a report? I think not.

Having too many pieces of paper is a disaster. Tim could never keep the cards straight and would find himself repeating information from various sources because he had too much information in too many places. We had the same problem with color coding folders and notebooks. Too much paper, too much clutter, and too much stress.

Together, using examples of his strengths and how his organizational deficits are roadblocks to success, we were able to advocate tossing the note cards and using the computer to do notes, outlines, and organizing. Bless the person who invented cut-and-paste and word-processing programs. With these tools, a previously impossible task is manageable.

We tried to follow the school's way of organizing and planning, but it never worked, and I got tired of Tim's being accused of not doing his work just because he lost it. He did it—he just didn't know where it was. Since I struggle with these same difficulties, I understood why this was such a problem. Finally, we accepted that we just have to be who we are and organize ourselves in the way that works for us.

My youngest son, Tom, should belong to Nancy. He is very organized. In his tackle box, his lures are sorted by size, type, and color. Everything is in its place. His schoolbag is also neat, and he flourishes in a clearly structured environment where he knows exactly what to expect. He often becomes frustrated with me when I can't find a permission slip. (I've warned him not to give them to me until I can sit down, look at them, and immediately return them.) Now that our daughter is married and he has his own room, he can organize to his heart's content.

My husband, Nick, and our daughter, Nicole, are also very organized. They write lists and stick to them. Nick and Tom work together well. They approach tasks the same way. Nick's fishing tackle is as neat as Tom's. Friends in his bass club are always threatening to dump his tackle box in the lake. Is it normal for a fisherman to be this organized? We won't bring up what mine and Tim's look like.

Needless to say, it gets interesting around our house. But we honor each other's diversity, and we learn from each other. Tim and I add a sense of creativity to the mix. Nick, Nicole, and Tom provide the structure and order. It's never boring.

Nancy's way

I am a part-to-whole learner and organizer. Everything has a place, and I need everything in its place. My home and office are very organized, and I can usually find things when I need them. (Sometimes I am so organized that I cannot find things within my system.)

I am very structured and organized in the way I approach and plan tasks. I begin with a mental image of the finished product, then organize in a step-by-step, sequential manner to reach that end. Mentally, I think through how I want to complete the project. I often shift the order in which things are to be accomplished until I have a comfortable and workable sequence. Then I either write an outline to follow or make a list of the steps in sequential order. My strong material-organization skills help me to have all my materials available at the workplace before I begin a task.

Then, piece by piece, I begin to put my plan in motion. Those who know me often hear me talk about getting all the pieces of the puzzle before the finished product appears. Whether painting a room or writing a book, I organize what needs to be done first, second, and so on until the task is completed as I mentally perceived it.

I use lists and planners to help me use my time efficiently. I am most productive in the morning, so I set aside that time to do any writing that needs to be accomplished. I am a better problem solver in the morning and am most effective in early morning meetings. Afternoons and evenings are when I accomplish menial tasks or chores and set aside time to relax and unwind.

I find that writing down things I need to remember removes the stress of having to rely on my memory. In the hectic pace of my day, with so much information coming at me at once, I am always afraid I will forget something important. Therefore, if I write down things I need to remember, my ideas are safe, and I think about something else. My daily planner and desk calendars are the backup systems I use to help my brain.

Being this organized has its drawbacks. I often appear rigid and inflexible. Transition and change are very difficult for me. Juggling too many things at once causes concern about the quality of what I am producing. However, out of necessity, I have had to learn to manage these factors. Doing one thing in isolation and bringing it to conclusion before I begin another is not realistic. Therefore, I set priorities, list them, and work from there until I accomplish my tasks. When I have to shift those priorities, I become overwhelmed and need to use self-talk to get reoriented.

I am a lot more flexible today than I was when Christian was born. It took about two days to realize that this child was different from his sister, and the way I was approaching him was not going to work. As the years passed, I had to become more flexible in how I managed Christian. I had to learn to pick my battles. Eventually, I began to understand. Christian is like Darlene in that he is a very global thinker. He sees the whole picture, and details are bothersome. Once I realized this, I was able to come to terms with the fact that Christian's way of organizing his personal space was chaos to me, but there was an organizational system. I gave up trying to impose my standards upon him. This also helped me to relax some of the pressure I placed on myself. I realized that my house did not need to be perfect, and if I did not dust every week, the dust would still be there when I got to it. I learned there are more important and enjoyable ways to spend my time.

While Christian helped me to be more relaxed about the organization of his personal space, I nonetheless insisted there be a strong structure to his household responsibilites and school activities. This structure has taught him the organizational skills necessary to function in society. While his method of organization is different from mine, he does have the skills he needs to complete his college courses and function in the workplace.

In other words, Christian has learned from me the organizational skills he needs to function in society, and I've learned to relax the demands I place on myself and enjoy life a little more. In this way, his ADD has had a very positive effect on my life.

Family Organization

Up to now we've thought or talked about organization as a way of keeping our environment in order and a way of approaching tasks. Organization is nothing more than a system or way of describing how something is structured. Color coding is a system for keeping books together. Time management is a system for studying.

Although it may not be immediately apparent, all families have some type of organization. Traditionally, structure was based on the two-parent family in which Dad went to work and Mom was a stay-at-home care provider. Dad brought home the bacon, as the saying goes, and Mom was responsible for school communications and keeping the family working as a cohesive unit. Things have changed. Today many women are single mothers, carrying the full burden of providing for the family's needs. Single fathers sometimes head households, and some children are raised by their grandparents.

Today, families must strive to be a whole functioning unit, often without many outside supports. Single parenthood and the lack of an extended family place enormous stress on the family, especially those with members who have ADD.

The popular mythology is that because family members live in close proximity, they think alike, feel alike, and want alike. Nothing could be further from the truth. Differences and disagreements are to be expected, because each person is unique and different.

Disagreement can actually help a family grow, as family members face their conflicts and work things out. We should strive to use these unique qualities and differences to figure out what type of organization works best for our family and how we can coordinate obligations so that each member feels like a contributor.

As our family and children grow, we strive to become a functioning whole of interdependent and independent parts. We are interdependent in that if one member has a problem, the entire family is affected. A parent loses a job, a child fails a grade, a family member becomes ill, and the delicate balance that is the family organization is

Figure 6–1
Family Organization

Task or Decision	Who Is Responsible	Why?

disrupted. Family members are independent in that we each leave our family, if only for a few hours a day, and function as autonomous human beings or as part of another system. We have our own hobbies, jobs, and activities we pursue outside of our family system.

Families grow and change, and so do the roles each member of the family is expected to fulfill. What we expect of a child when they are five years old is vastly different from their role in the family at fifteen.

In order to become a whole unit, families, whatever their form, must learn how to work together, solve problems, and plan. That can be quite a challenge. Think about your family. How is it organized? Who is responsible for which tasks? How did you arrive at this decision? If relationships are rocky and tasks are left undone, think about assigning tasks using a strengths perspective.

Does the person who loves animals the most take care of the dog? If one child loves to cook, let him plan dinner every Wednesday night.

Use the chart (Figure 6-1) to help you understand who makes decisions or does chores and jobs in your family and why. Are you using each family member's strengths? If not, you might consider reassigning tasks or allowing everyone involved to participate in the decision-making process.

When this happens, each family member becomes a partner in finding solutions, performing jobs or chores, and building skills. If you are unsure of how to go about involving your family in this process, look at family meetings in the communication section.

Building skills in such areas as communication, problem solving, and organization helps us and our children meet the world on an even level. Without these skills, our children may suffer socially. No one will see all the wonderful talents and strengths they possess. As difficult as the academic and social struggles are, they can be overcome. The child who finds it difficult making and keeping friends may derive particular benefit from skill building as an avenue to creating long-lasting friendships.

Wanted: Just One Friend!

Not being accepted by one's peers is a painful experience. You may recall a time when you were the only one in the class not invited to a party or always the last one chosen for the team. Everyone has experienced being socially isolated at one time or another.

However, for children with ADD, ostracism can be a way of life. These are the children who want and need friends yet unwittingly alienate their peers. Watching your child be excluded and being unable to help is a painful experience.

"Social skills" is a term not all of us exactly understand, although we hear it often. A child demonstrating appropriate social skills is polite and well-mannered, responds appropriately in a conversation, reads the nonverbal cues of those around him, stops and thinks before acting, and can read a social situation and decide what actions or responses are needed. For example, if the teacher is angry because of a problem on the playground, the child with appropriate social skills knows to look remorseful and sit quietly and listen.

Children with developed social skills know the social rules and usually follow them. They have learned how to take turns both in conversation and in play. They share easily and have some degree of negotiating and problem-solving skill.

In his video *Last One Picked, First One Picked On,* Richard Lavoie discusses the result of a study that surveyed children to find out what they liked about other children. The children who appeal to other children

> Smile and laugh
> Greet others
> Extend invitations
> Converse
> Share
> Give compliments
> Have a neat appearance.

Interestingly, when teachers were asked to list the traits they like about their students, they did not include academic ability. The attributes teachers did list were students who were

> Punctual
> Established eye contact
> Participated in class
> Used the teacher's name
> Submitted work on time
> Used required formats
> Erased and rewrote rather than scratched out information
> Requested explanations
> Thanked the teacher after class.

Children with ADD usually do not possess these qualities. They are unable to pick up on the subtleties in what Lavoie refers to as the "hidden curriculum." Studies suggest that as many as 80 percent of all children with ADD experience some type of social difficulty. For many of these children, social interaction may be further hampered by a language impairment.

Often children with poor social skills appear to function better in a more structured environment such as the classroom. However, in open, overstimulating situations like the playground, lunchroom, or soccer field, they lose control. Often these open situations become so stressful children purposely act out to avoid being placed there. It is not uncommon for children to find ways to receive the "punishment" of missing recess so they can avoid going out. Unfinished work or missing homework assignments are often used by students for this purpose.

Being less mature, they often appear bossy, silly, or babyish in their play. Children with ADD may be as much as 20 percent behind their classmates in the development of their social skills. For this reason, they are more comfortable with younger playmates whom they may be able to dominate and control.

The impulsivity and hyperactivity of young children with ADD often worries and confuses their playmates. Peers are overwhelmed by their exuberance. If their speech is delayed, there is difficulty being understood and communicating, and this adds to the problem of social interaction.

The symptoms of the disorder continue to interfere with the child's ability to make friends after he enters school. Disruptions in the classroom and on the playground result in children with ADD being labeled as having behavior problems, and classmates avoid them. Impulsive and hyperactive children find it difficult to wait their turn. Their inability to focus may cause them to break the rules of the game, or they make mistakes that cause further alienation and frustration for everyone involved. A child on third base creating a dust storm rather than attending to the ball and the runner heading toward him may be responsible for a run scored by the other team. Angered by everyone's yelling at him, he loses his temper and lashes out, and a fight ensues.

Language can continue to be an issue if the child miscues or has problems processing conversations quickly enough to remain an active participant. Children often enjoy playing with words as they learn the use of more complex sentence structures. The child who does not understand jokes or the subtleties of conversational language, such as puns, may become the object of the humor.

As children get older, their need for social interaction increases, and a lack of social skills becomes more apparent. As adolescents attempt to move away from their parents and establish their own autonomy, they turn toward their peers. An adolescent with ADD who has not learned the social rules is at great risk. In an effort to gain peer acceptance, the teen may get involved in high-risk behaviors such as drugs, alcohol, delinquency, or speeding. Desiring acceptance, he may develop friendships with other children like himself, children who are on the outside looking in.

Finding his niche becomes increasingly difficult. Academically, poor organizational and listening skills add to the frustration. As the work load and demands increase, the student lacking these skills falls farther and farther behind. Frustration mounts and failure looms. Gaining peer acceptance through academic achievement is not realistic. Instead, such children become known as the "dumb" kids or the "retards."

Many parents encourage organized sports as a way to provide social contacts for their children. Many children with ADD appear clumsy and have less developed motor skills than their peers. Also, the hallmark characteristics of ADD may interfere with the child's ability to be a team player.

If your child is interested in playing on a team, begin by considering his strengths (you may want to pull out his strengths balance sheet) and how the ADD affects him. If possible, investigate the requirements of the sport and the expectations of the coach. For sports to offer a successful social experience for your child, a match between your child's strengths and the sport he chooses is very important.

If your child has poor eye-hand coordination and is a daydreamer, Little League may not be a good choice. However, if he moves with the grace of a gazelle and has boundless energy, a fast-paced sport such as soccer may be a great match.

Keep in mind that many children with ADD find individualized sports such as swimming, track, or horseback riding very rewarding. They still benefit from having the chance to get rid of excess energy in a directed, organized way, and they have the social contact with other children on their team.

Participation in athletics can be a very positive way to allow your child to shine in front of his peers. A sport that utilizes his strengths and abilities could help him develop new friendships and social acceptance. A successful sporting experience may build confidence and help him to feel like one of the crowd.

Often children with ADD feel very different, and this increases their anxiety around their peers. Awareness of having a disability can be very traumatic for a youngster (and the parents!). That is why it is essential that the child, the family, and the teachers become informed. There are excellent books available in local bookstores or through mail order explaining ADD to children and adolescents. In the bibliography at the back of this book, we have listed a few of these books. The information they offer will help your child understand that "different" is a quality adding to the beauty of who he or she is.

Parents can further help their child develop social skills.

1. Maintain medication during participation in sports or social activities.
2. As discussed in the section on communication, get a language evaluation, and therapy if your child is language-impaired.
3. Develop social scripts with your child. Model and role-play to practice social interactions. For example, how would your child act at a birthday party? At a Scout meeting? At the movies?
4. Help your child learn to solve problems by practicing different social situations that might arise during the day. For example, if someone teases him, what would he do? If he got into trouble, how would he explain the situation to the teacher? The principal? The school nurse?

5. Help your child entertain friends. Begin with one friend coming to visit. Rehearse how to greet the guest. Give your child ideas on what activities may be available. Have a secret signal to use when your child needs reminding of appropriate behavior or to regain control. For example, a tug on the ear may work.

6. Find ways to minimize your child's weaknesses by building on her strengths. Sharing common interests is the first step to developing friendships. If your child cannot successfully participate in team sports, consider individual sports, such as swimming or track. Maybe your child's dance class or drama club may be where she can excel and find social acceptance. No one is good at everything, but we are all good at something!

Social acceptance is critical to how we perceive ourselves. Rejection can be devastating. All the topics discussed in this section of the book are interrelated. They cannot be isolated. The development of communication skills is a part of organization and problem solving. If you cannot communicate and solve problems in a methodical, organized way, you may appear socially offensive.

The final section of this manual will address how the development of these skills can be used to strengthen the character and well-being of the child with attention deficit disorder.

PART THREE

Overcoming Roadblocks to Success

7

Judgmental Statements

Parents can learn about ADD, identify their children's strengths, and teach their children the skills needed to be successful—and still, just when you think things are going OK, someone tosses an obstacle into the middle of the road. Have no fear. Even the most skilled navigators have to make an occasional detour. Just knowing these roadblocks are a possibility gives you the power to get past them.

One of the biggest obstacles to success for children with ADD is the damage to their self-esteem. Most often this occurs through judgmental statements.

Advice abounds. Well-meaning relatives, neighbors, and teachers are filled with advice about how to fix your child. Grandpa might shake his head and mutter, "If I had that kid for a week, I'd set him straight." Be stricter, be more patient, be more structured, be flexible. What is a parent to do? Everywhere are constant reminders that our child is less than perfect and not-so-subtle reminders that we aren't such great parents either. It's so easy to blame Mom or Dad. We are visible targets, and ADD is a disorder hard to pinpoint. It's even easier to blame the child.

Her name seems to be the only one spoken in class. "Connie, get your book out. Connie, shut your desk. Connie, start your work. Connie, pay attention. Connie, if you don't finish your work you will sit in class at recess."

This constant reminding of deficits often encourages peers to shy away from a child, or worse, to imitate the behavior the authority figure has modeled. Connie becomes the scapegoat for everything that happens in and outside of class.

Few adults realize that children with ADD would give anything to be able to stay out of trouble, to be on the honor roll, to be recognized for some achievement or act of kindness, and to be in control.

Sometimes it is even difficult for family members, friends, and neighbors to accept the diagnosis of ADD. They may observe that the child is reckless and label him destructive, never recognizing the child has a problem with impulsiveness. Children who are easily distracted may be labeled dizzy. Children who have trouble completing tasks may be labeled lazy. Complicating all this is the hallmark of ADD, inconsistent performance. Teachers, relatives, and neighbors observe a child being careful, listening, following rules, or completing a task once and they logically assume the child is capable of doing these things consistently. When the child's inconsistencies surface, he is thought to be choosing not to comply.

Probably the most maddening judgmental statement is any that includes the word *responsibility*. It seems children's lives are filled with people telling them to be more responsible. They must be responsible for their homework and for asking the teacher to help them. It's their responsibility to always know what needs to be done and when. And they must at all times be responsible for their behavior, regardless of outside distractions or what others do.

It has always been a source of real amazement to Darlene how many schools are resistant to providing to children with ADD or learning difficulties a list of assignments or upcoming tests. Most schools insist the child write assignments in their assignment book and bring the book to the teacher for review and signature at the end of each class.

This makes the child responsible for making sure he knows the course requirements, and if he misses an assignment, he has no one to blame but himself. This can be useful if the goal is to ensure the child has written the assignments correctly.

The problems arise when children are shy, intimidated by the teacher, or unable to discern when it is appropriate to approach the teacher. Children with poor organizational skills may also need more time to get from class to class. Using transition time to have the teacher review assignment notebooks may place the disorganized child in the position of playing catch-up as he moves from class to class, always a little behind.

The funny thing is we that have yet to encounter a college teacher who does not provide a syllabus at the beginning of each quarter or semester, detailing reading assignments, papers and projects due, and the date of each test. All this is provided for adults, and the adults who benefit from these detailed syllabuses are not seen as irresponsible. It's illogical.

The admonishments to be responsible may continue in the college years. School administrators may regard any request for modification or waiver of requirements because of ADD or learning difficulties as a student's attempt to escape fulfilling his responsibilities.

It seems a common belief that children have this magic "responsibility" gene that just turns on when they enter the fourth, fifth, or seventh grade, or whatever the magic number is in your neck of the woods. If there is such a gene, we know there are millions of parents who would love to know how to activate it.

At a "get to know the teacher" meeting, a fourth-grade teacher tersely announced to parents that they were not to help their children with homework. "This is about taking the responsibility off the parents and putting the responsibility on the child," proclaimed the teacher as she continued to name all the ways children would now be responsible. The parents present where apprised of a list of possible punishments their children could receive for not fulfilling these awesome responsibilities. The parents were intimidated. They meekly left the room, feeling a little sick about the upcoming year and dreading the consequences of so much responsibility.

We acknowledge that it is essential to teach responsibility. This book is about helping your child discover his strengths and develop the skills to obtain this admirable trait. The question is, When and how much responsibility? Even children without any special challenges develop and mature at varying rates. The child's stage of development, level of skills, and the extent of his support system all need to be considered when deciding when and how much responsibility he can handle. Unrealistic expectations are a real roadblock to a child's success.

There is so much pressure for children to conform that parents also fall into the trap of placing unrealistic expectations on them. Parents get frustrated and use the same judgmental statements we resent others using.

Have you said unkind words to your child in the last week? Use Figure 7-1 to make a list of situations where your child pushed your buttons and record how you responded. If you find yourself making impulsive statements, make another list of alternative ways of handling the situations when they occur again. If you find this difficult, refer back to the communication section and to "I" statements.

Figure 7–1
List of Judgmental Statements

Judgmental statements:

_____

_____

_____

_____

Alternative statements:

_____

_____

_____

_____

The Need to Know

Parents may choose not to disclose to neighbors or friends the fact that their child has ADD. This decision depends on how close they are to the family and on how often the child must interact with them. Often parents receive negative feedback from those who view any explanation as a parent's desire to blame a disorder, instead of the child, for problems that occur.

Of course it is the parents' decision whom to tell and what to say. Obviously those who are in daily contact with a child will benefit from knowing and understanding how his ADD is manifested. Day-care providers and parents of a child's close friends probably should know. Parents do not need to describe every detail of the disorder to every acquaintance. Helping others understand your child can deter those damaging judgmental statements.

Today's climate is sometimes stormy when it comes to ADD. We hear stories of troubled teens committing crimes or dropping out of school and ADD is used as the excuse. ADD is never an excuse. But it can be an explanation.

Use your communication skills to teach those with whom your child interacts that knowledge is prevention and not intended as an excuse. Let us stress two points. First, the best prevention is intervention. The earlier intervention takes place, the more likely a child will develop skills and strengths to protect him from high-risk behaviors. Second, the absence of appropriate intervention can leave a child with ADD vulnerable to outside pressure.

When you are dealing with Sunday-school teachers, coaches, or others not in daily contact with your child, you can afford to be selective in what you share. Instead of mentioning ADD, you might just name the symptoms (tell a coach, for example, your child has always been easily distractable and needs lots of action to keep him interested). Tell the Sunday-school teacher your child is fidgety and will benefit from being allowed to kneel in her seat or stand at the art table.

One guideline: The teacher must be told. A teacher probably spends more time with a child than does the family. It is imperative a child's teacher be aware of all the ways ADD can be manifested and how to identify when she is seeing symptoms of ADD or a learning disability and when the problem is something else. Remember, most teachers have not been trained in how to identify ADD or how to teach a child with ADD. They are getting on-the-job training too.

Children are continually developing, and each stage of development brings new challenges. Keep your balance sheet (the one you created in part 1 of this book) up to date and share your insights with your child's teacher.

In spite of all the information parents might provide to teachers, they sometimes fall into the trap of looking at outcomes and making moral judgments. This is discouraging to the child, but it can be an opportunity to clear another roadblock.

Education Opportunities

Recently an eighth grader, John, failed a history test. The teacher wrote in bold red letters across the paper: "Study. You will have to know this information. You will never graduate from high school until you know this." Thanks for sharing those motivating thoughts.

Failing one or even several tests in elementary school does not mean automatic failure in high school. How a child's teacher perceives him, and the not-so-subtle messages the teacher sends, can be very real roadblocks to success.

Frankie was twelve when the teacher sent a paper home to be signed by his parents. "Sloppy" was written in bold red letters across the paper. "Frankie does not take the time to do his work neatly" was written across the bottom. "Redo."

The teacher was describing symptoms of ADD (impulsiveness) and the results of Frankie's written language disability and difficulty with fine motor skills. In fact, he had spent hours the previous night preparing the "sloppy" paper. His parents wrote a nonjudgmental letter, using "I" statements, describing their sympathy with the teacher in her distress over Frankie's inability to write well. Of course, they wrote, they were sure she was aware that this was a manifestation of his learning disabilities and ADD, and they did appreciate her patience in the matter.

Eventually Frankie learned to use a word processor, and now he prepares presentable papers. His handwriting still resembles something from an ancient Egyptian tomb. But, now a high school student, he is able to do most of his written work using a computer. Finally, the quality of his written output represents his ability.

Sara's mom was continually frustrated by Sara's teachers' lack of understanding. Sara got straight *A*s in math, but inattention to detail was causing her problems in science. It was difficult for Sara's teacher to understand how Sara could get straight *A*s in math and nearly fail science. The only logical answer was that Sara just didn't like science and didn't *want* to do it. As a result, the worse Sara did on tests and papers, the harder the teacher was on her, keeping her in from recess and sending notes home to her parents detailing all the deficits she possessed.

Luckily Sara's mom had a balance sheet highlighting the symptoms of ADD that were a problem for Sara. She shared this information, along with Sara's strengths. Together, she and the teacher went over Sara's balance sheet. Mom had prepared excerpts from the literature she read and underlined the parts illustrating Sara's difficulties. She had expert testimony explaining why Sara wasn't excelling in science. Sara, her mother, and the teacher set reachable goals for Sara in science.

Perhaps the teacher still believed Sara's problem was due to some moral lack on Sara's part, but faced with facts and a solid plan, she was at least willing to set aside her beliefs and give Sara the benefit of the doubt.

Right now, you are probably saying, "Right, I can do all that." Yes, you can. Every time you read an article or part of a book and find symptoms of your child described, copy that section, highlight it, and save it. Save samples of your child's work, especially handwriting. If your child takes medication, keep samples of work done both on and off medication.

Also keep copies of all testing results, IEPs, conference reports, and any other material documenting your child's learning difficulties. Record manifestations of ADD symptoms, as well as strategies that have been successful in the past. Keep this information in chronological order and you will always have your evidence handy and ready to use when you need supporting documents.

In the problem-solving section, we talked about the ways change takes place. One way is through education. That is your goal. The next time unrealistic expectations are placed on your child, gather your evidence, educate, and advocate for fair (not equal) treatment and fair goals for your child.

Do not overload your teachers with mountains of literature, but provide a general overview of your child's strengths and weaknesses at the beginning of the year and then address particular issues as they arise.

Let us say we're not picking on teachers. The facts are that the school environment is often not a user-friendly one for the child with ADD. Parents who are frustrated by their school's inability or unwillingness to help their child outnumber those who are thrilled by the help their child is getting. This does not mean there aren't many dedicated, loving teachers who inspire and nourish children with ADD. There are! These teachers honor the child who marches to the beat of a different drummer.

Darlene's youngest child wouldn't have survived the first grade if not for the love and dedication of his teacher, Mrs. Waddell. She constantly told all her "smart cookies" how wonderful they were. She was affirming, patient, and encouraging. She made learning challenging, fun, and obtainable. If only we could have cloned her, or promoted her through the eighth grade!

There is a Charlie Brown cartoon where Charlie is glowing over a remark made by his teacher. "It's always great to be recognized in your own lifetime," Charlie is saying. Truer words were never spoken, and the teacher who can recognize and appreciate children who walk their own path is a treasure.

One teacher commented that it was always exciting to watch Bobby learn a new concept in science, because he always came to an idea through the back door. This teacher saw the free association of ideas and the mental distractibility that annoy some and encouraged their use as an alternative way of learning and problem solving. It really is great to be recognized in your own lifetime!

Don't wait for a crisis to educate those with whom your child interacts. Once a crisis occurs, everyone is too emotionally involved to be open to creative solutions. If you see a fire smoldering, put it out. Don't wait for it to become a four-alarm blaze.

Choosing Your Battles

Several years ago Kenny Rogers performed the song *The Gambler.* The song's advice is that you need to know when to hold 'em and when to fold 'em. Deciding which battles to fight isn't an easy task. You have to know which battles are worth the fight and when to fold. Ask yourself the following questions when deciding which battles to fight.

- How will my child's life be better or different if I fight this battle?
- What is the worst thing that will happen if I don't intervene?
- What am I willing to do to change things?
- Is it really possible for me to change the situation?
- What are my options?
- What are the consequences?

Up to now, we have assumed that the battles you are fighting are for your child, and the world is the foe. But what happens when your adversary is your child? Pretty much the same thing. You have to decide which battles to fight and when to go with the flow. Many children with ADD have a very low frustration tolerance. This trait can cause problems socially, at school, and in the family. When things are difficult or roadblocks get in your child's way, he may blow a fuse.

The key in preventing these situations or keeping them from getting out of control is deciding which are important.

In the real world, it probably doesn't matter if your child does fifteen math problems now and ten later, or studies spelling and then does his reading work sheet. It won't matter if he studies at 3:14 or 5:30. What matters is that the work is completed.

So save the big guns for the big battles. If your child's actions will hurt him or someone else, intervention is necessary. If no one will be hurt, you might choose to allow your child to proceed and learn from his or her actions. This will help your child learn that every action has consequences, good or bad, and that responsibility must be taken for those actions. It can also send the message that you love your child enough to allow him or her to occasionally make mistakes. If you teach your child that situations are negotiable, he can learn the valuable skill of problem solving. He is also more likely to respect your stand when you do make it. He will have learned valuable life lessons.

The Fragile Treasure: Your Child's Spirit

In the beginning of this book, we referred to children with ADD as diamonds in the rough. All children can glitter; some just need more polishing than others. Psychologist Carl Rogers wrote that all human beings deserve to be treated with unconditional positive regard. Nowhere is this more true and necessary than when working or living with children with ADD. Unconditional positive regard means that although we may not like certain behaviors, we still love our children. They have value. They are our treasures.

All children need to know they are valued. Whether they believe this depends on the input they receive from those around them. As parents, we need to ensure that our child's spirit is nourished with honest and sincere statements of value. An easy way to send your child this message is by accentuating the positive things he does.

Below are some ideas to help you and your child focus on the positive. A warning needs to be issued here. Many of these ideas may sound ideal for your situation and easy to implement. However, if you and your child are deeply entrenched in the negative cycle, finding something positive could be challenging.

In the beginning you may find yourself digging very deep to find something positive. These positives don't necessarily have to be big accomplishments or tasks completed. You can give your child a warm smile or a hug and say, "You know, I've always thought you had the most beautiful brown eyes. They are so warm and inviting." Telling your teenage son this might bring a response of "Leave me alone" or just a cold stare, but when he thinks you aren't looking, you might notice his step has just a little more spring to it.

We've used the word *spirit* because it implies more than just a good feeling about oneself. It implies something deeper—a profound belief of worth and an understanding of who you are and your place in the world. Children (and adults) lacking a strong sense of themselves may be vulnerable to outside pressures or judgmental statements and adopt unhealthy coping strategies, such as substance abuse. So get ready to accentuate the positives in your live and your child's.

1. There is no better place to start than with your child's name. You picked his name for a reason. Was there a person you admired? What does his name mean? How does that relate to who he is? Thomas means "seeker of truth." What a perfect name for a hyperactive, curious young boy. Tom's scrapbook begins with a picture of Tommy climbing out of his crib. Underneath this picture is "Thomas, seeker of truth." He gets a kick out of this every time he opens his scrapbook. His sense of adventure and his need to understand why is acknowledged. He has never been one to follow meekly. He is always on the go, always seeking. He is truly Thomas. What is your child's name? What does it mean? What positive things do you see in your child each day? Share them with your child.

2. Make a "positive book." This can be a great home-school communication tool if you involve the teacher (who also needs

to begin looking at the positive qualities in your child). A positive book can be a notebook or journal that your child makes or chooses. Each day, you enter something positive about your child. Then your child makes a positive entry about something he did. The teacher can also make a school entry. This book gives a written account of the positive side of your child. On days when positive encouragement is needed by you, your child, or the teacher, this book serves as a reference to show the many positive qualities your child possesses.

3. Use mealtime to discuss something positive that happened to each family member during the day. This is a nice focus for the dinner hour and sets a good tone for the evening.

4. Don't tie positives only to accomplishments. Leave love notes and/or messages for your child even when he hasn't done anything special. What a day brightener to find a note from home in the lunch box or schoolbag. Look for every opportunity to let him know you are glad he is part of your family. Darlene uses the marquee screen saver in her computer software to send quirky messages to her kids. In turn they send love letters back: "Mom is really, really goofy and we are not lying." You never know what you'll find if the computer is idle for more than a minute.

5. Thank your child when you notice him cooperating or helping another child. Some children have difficulty seeing another's point of view. Praising them for acts of kindness lets them know you value these actions. Children who struggle can be very empathic to others' suffering. Reinforce this empathy as a valued trait.

6. Use the sandwich technique when negatives must be addressed. Begin with a positive statement, sandwich in the negative, and end with another positive. For example: You did a great job washing the dishes. You forgot washing the countertop is part of that job. Clean it and you will be finished and can go out to play. Thanks, I appreciate your help!

Pointing out the positives help children develop a strong sense of self. The ideas above can be very effective in pulling families together. Somehow you become so involved focusing on the positives that negatives get minimized. This positive focus serves as a reminder that we all have something worthwhile to offer, especially the child with ADD. What a terrific way to protect your child from roadblocks to success.

8

Risk-Taking Behavior

Children take risks. Children with ADD are no exception. In fact, some parents of children with ADD consider their children experts at risk taking. Their hair-raising adventures give the strongest parent weak knees. They build ramps and jump over obstacles on their bikes. They have no fear of ten-foot-high diving boards or fifteen feet of water.

"I had a real adventure," reported mud-covered Tom to his mom. "You know that big cliff at Clough Creek? Well, I jumped it and missed and I had to grab a branch from a bush so I didn't fall on the rock and I had to crawl up the side of the cliff and that's how I got mud all over me," said Tom in one long breath with a big smile on his face. Mom let out a long sigh.

A little adventure is good for kids. They learn problem-solving skills and how to work with others. Overcoming obstacles gives them confidence. This kind of risk taking is growth.

Some risk taking doesn't promote growth. Risk taking in this category involves experimentation with alcohol and other drugs, juvenile delinquency, and other self-destructive behaviors. A child whose ADD is not managed early and who enters adolescence with difficulties in major life areas is especially at risk for these kinds of problems.

Adolescence does not have to be a time of strife and struggle. Contrary to some commonly held beliefs, most young people manage the transition of adolescence without serious problems.

Many of the adolescent behaviors that give this age group such a negative image are interrelated. School failure, delinquent or criminal behavior, alcohol and drug use, aggression or depression, and precocious sexual behavior are often coexisting. Most of these behaviors are concentrated within a relatively small and identifiable segment of the adolescent population.

Experimenting with Alcohol and Other Drugs

All children face decisions regarding experimenting with tobacco, alcohol, or other substances. The 1995 Monitoring the Future study indicates that illicit drug use by adolescents has increased in the last few years. This survey, sponsored by the National Institute on Drug Abuse, reflects attitudes and patterns of use for in-school adolescents.

According to the survey, alcohol, tobacco, and inhalants, in that order, are the substances most abused by eighth graders. Fifty-five percent of eight graders have tried alcohol. Forty-seven percent have used cigarettes. Nearly one in five eighth graders surveyed indicated they had used inhalants at least once. Marijuana use is also on the increase among youth. Twenty percent of eighth graders have used marijuana. Forty-two percent reported having used marijuana at least once by the time they were seniors.

These statistics represent use in the general population. What do they mean for our kids with ADD? Their risk is at least the same as the general population. For some the risk is greater.

Researchers are just beginning to study how ADD and alcoholism are related to each other, and whether individuals with AD/HD have a genetic predisposition to alcoholism. A look at the literature gives us a hint at this relationship. In his book *Tourette Syndrome and Human Behaviors,* David Comings gives an account of a 1981 study by J.R. Cloninger, M.D.

Dr. Cloninger did a detailed behavior assessment of 431 eleven-year-olds and reexamined them when they were twenty-seven. "This study showed that those children who ranked high in novelty seeking and low in avoiding harm were twenty times more likely to develop alcoholism as adults," Comings wrote.

Cloninger described novelty seekers as extremely overactive, unable to sit still, unable to concentrate, easily provoked, quick to lose their temper, and disruptive. Children who demonstrated a low avoidance of harm were described as overactive, highly uninhibited, distractible, and unconcerned with personal safety. It sounds a lot like a symptoms list of ADD, doesn't it?

These findings are not surprising since several studies have indicated that hyperactivity can be an early sign of predisposition to alcoholism. Hyperactive children are also more likely to have a history of alcoholism in the family.

A retrospective survey of hospitalized adult alcoholics at the University of Vermont showed that nearly half of these patients described childhood behavior problems resembling the symptoms of hyperactivity.

Of course, not everyone with AD/HD becomes alcoholic or chemically dependent, or vice versa. However, there does appear to be a subgroup of people with severe AD/HD or combined AD/HD and "conduct disorder" who appear to be especially susceptible to alcoholism. A history of chemical dependency in the family, school failure, and association with peers who use gateway drugs are also strong factors. Younger children may be more vulnerable because of lack of cognitive and social skills.

The good news is that individuals who develop healthy coping skills and learn to inhibit their behavior are at no greater risk than the general population. However, among untreated AD/HD adults and those without effective intervention, abuse is more common.

Alcohol and Other Drugs:
Alligators in the Roadway

Darlene's mother grew up in Florida during the depression. As a child, she loved exciting stories. A favorite concerned the "alligator announcements." Eustis, Florida, was not very developed then, and alligators had the right of way. School officials would keep track of any alligators spotted near the school and would announce their location before the end of the day. Children would be warned before the journey home. They knew where alligators were and what roads or paths to avoid. To have no contact with alligators is the low-risk choice—the only safe choice. Our personal bias regarding alcohol and other drug use is that no use is the best choice—the only safe choice.

We will not attempt to give a comprehensive report on drugs here. We do want to give a brief survey of the drugs most used by students and the special problems they may present for individuals with ADD. We will not cover tobacco. We assume you already know the risks associated with its use. We will say that many are convinced that early tobacco use is a factor leading to the use of other drugs. Tobacco is sometimes called a gateway drug, meaning it opens the door for future use of mind-altering substances. Like all other substances, the lowest-risk use is no use.

Most use begins with curiosity. Junior-high students may begin to experiment with mood-altering drugs. If the child experiences negative consequences at this point, he is less likely to continue using.

Many adolescents will continue social use and never go beyond that. Unfortunately, many are unable to maintain this level of use. Continued use may lead to preoccupation with the chemical and finally dependency.

Let us make it very clear. The use of alcohol and other drugs is not a normal part of growing up. Use should not be ignored. It will not go away as the child matures. Early use may be a red flag that other issues need immediate attention.

If your child chooses to experiment with drugs, he may get away with its use and escape consequences. The problem is that there is no way of knowing for sure who is at risk and who isn't. In short, there are no guarantees. Treatment centers and jails are filled with adults and adolescents who took the risk and lost.

Alcohol

Alcohol abuse is a major problem in America. According to government estimates, there are 10.5 million adults suffering from true alcohol dependency and an additional 7.2 million alcohol abusers. Alcohol problems cross all socioeconomic, gender, and racial lines. Its use is widely accepted despite the obvious negative consequences.

Part of the attraction for kids is the glamour the media attaches to drinking. The message is, Drinking makes you popular, happy, and successful. Children as young as fourth graders report being pressured to use alcohol. For the child with school and social difficulties, alcohol can appear to be the answer. Such children may use drugs to self-medicate or dull the emotional pain they are experiencing.

Alcohol may seem to make social situations easier, but alcohol is actually an anesthetic. It depresses the central nervous system. If a child's central nervous system is already functioning at a slower pace, it doesn't need to be depressed. The more alcohol consumed, the less inhibited the individual becomes. Motor skills and reasoning abilities may be impaired.

Impulsive behavior may result from low levels of certain neurotransmitters. What happens when alcohol is introduced? Further depletion of the neurotransmitter levels, which can lead to more impulsive behaviors. For the child who is hyperactive and impulsive, this is a prescription for trouble.

Legal consequences for underage drinking differ from state to state. Most states have lowered the blood alcohol concentration necessary for conviction to .02 percent. If an underage teen is convicted of driving after consumption, he may face fines or time in jail. The officer can take any property used in committing this crime, and it may not be returned.

Marijuana

This drug is used by a large cross section of American society. It's mind-boggling the number of people who still believe marijuana is a harmless drug. The facts indicate otherwise.

There are over 400 chemicals in marijuana. The chemical that gets people high (or mellow) is THC (delta-9 tetrahydrocannabinol). This chemical affects people in various ways, but the impact it has on learning is universal.

THC changes the way information gets into the part of the brain scientists believe controls memory. Research has indicated that marijuana interferes with short-term memory, especially memory of those things learned through sight or sound. Users might not remember actions taken or things done. More frightening, they may not be aware of the memory loss. Within hours of using, concentration may decrease. There can be a distorted sense of the passage of time, and the more complex reflexes are slowed. Continued use can result in amotivational syndrome, characterized by general lethargy—loss of interest in work, school, relationships, and other life areas. It doesn't take much imagination to figure out what an impact this drug can have on the child or adult with ADD. Attention, motivation, memory, and the ability to stay with a task may be seriously impacted.

Users fall into the trap of thinking occasional use is without risk. Once again, the facts indicate otherwise. THC has a half-life of three days. This means that if you smoke a joint on Monday, half of the chemical will still be in your body on Thursday. It can be detected in urine up to thirty days after use. Urine is water-based, something THC doesn't like. Imagine how long it stays in the fatty tissues, such as the brain, where it is stored. Since it doesn't leave the body quickly, using even a few times a week will result in accumulation of THC in the body. As use continues, a reservoir of THC builds up in the fatty tissues. Even after a person stops using, he is affected by the drug for quite some time. In heavy users, it can take months or even years for all the THC to leach out of the fatty tissues.

Once again, this can cause a terrible problem for the young person with ADD who is already experiencing school problems. Just when he reaches a stage in his academic life when he needs to be able to remember, focus, and stick to a task, experimenting with marijuana becomes a major stumbling block to success.

Inhalant abuse

Young people are likely to abuse inhalants because of their availability. Inhalants are vapors that produce mind-altering effects. Most garages or basements or offices contain substances that could be abused.

Inhalants fall into three main categories: gases, solvents, and nitrites. Gases can be found in household items such as spray paints, butane lighters, aerosols, and fabric protector sprays. Solvents are found in items such as paint thinners, solvents, gasoline, and glues. Such office supplies as correction fluids and felt-tip markers also fall into this category. Nitrites can be found in over-the-counter room deodorizers.

The adverse effects of use can be tragic and final. More than one news report has covered the death of a young person from sniffing paint or glue. High concentrations of the chemicals in solvents or aerosol sprays can induce heart failure resulting in death. High concentrations of inhalants can also cause suffocation by displacing oxygen in the lungs and then in the central nervous system.

Inhaling solvents can also cause hearing loss, brain damage, liver and kidney damage, bone marrow damage, and other irreversible problems.

Sometimes curious children unintentionally misuse inhalants found around the house. This could be an issue for the impulsive, risk-taking child with ADD. Parents must closely monitor these substances and educate children about the hazards of even unintentional misuse. Never assume your children are learning the risk from school or other sources. Always focus on the safe use of these products, the danger of misuse, and the need for a well-ventilated area whenever use is necessary.

Ritalin

Does using Ritalin or other stimulant medications place a child at higher risk for substance abuse? The research indicates it does not. Face it! Some kids will use and abuse substances. Some kids will take anything they can get their hands on. News reports of kids crushing and sniffing Ritalin or injecting it are scary. Fortunately, most kids who have ADD and who take Ritalin or other stimulants are not abusing their medication.

There are certainly cases of abuse. However, those abusing Ritalin may be taking ten times the prescribed dosage. Adults can prevent abuses by closely monitoring their child's medication. Medications should not be left lying around on countertops, in cars, or in purses.

At school, medications should be keep in the nurse's office, under supervision. If a school nurse is not on-site, medications should be kept in the office in a locked area, such as a desk drawer or a locker. Common sense can reduce availability and prevent abuse.

There are no national statistics from the Drug Enforcement Agency on how much Ritalin has been diverted from intended use. These records are kept at the local level. The DEA states the reason that Ritalin abuse is not a big issue is because it is a controlled substance. Local police officers indicate that in nearly all cases, diversion is committed by adults, not children. Parents have diagnosed their own ADD and taken their children's medication. Parents have used Ritalin as a diet aid or to help stay awake. It is a felony to possess another person's medication. If you suspect you have ADD, get a diagnosis and proper treatment.

Prevention

Sooner or later your child will probably be exposed to drugs. Parents are the key to a child's growing up drug-free. Parents can help children learn the life skills necessary to protect the whole child.

The whole child involves physical, cognitive, and spiritual development. Good nutrition, plenty of rest, and exercise help develop a strong physical self. Encouragement, supportive teachers, bypass strategies, remediation, structure, and flexibility are among the tools needed to achieve cognitive growth. The spiritual part of the child is probably the most important. Alcoholics Anonymous has a saying that spirituality is the first thing to go with alcoholism and the last thing to come back. To develop life skills in all these areas, children need to learn how to:

Handle frustration.

Teach stress management through exercise, rest, leisure activities, and breathing activities.

Express feelings.

Feelings tucked inside aren't resolved. Teach your child to express himself and listen to others without letting emotions cloud the issues.

Solve problems.

How to say no; how to stop and think; what to do when you see a friend use; how to handle situations that could get you into trouble! These are all skills children need to learn.

Communicate.

Communication is more than expressing and understanding feelings. This is how kids learn to get what they need. As you learned earlier, won't receive unless you ask.

Think positive thoughts.

How we think affects how we feel, and how we feel affects how we act. Children who think, "I am loved, I am competent, I am worthwhile," will be less likely to turn to drugs when they have a problem.

Parents can contribute to skill development by following tips presented in the previous sections of this book. Parents also need to be role models. Don't practice "Do what I say, not what I do." Kids will do what we do. If you truly want your child to be drug-free, model that behavior. If you drink, drink responsibly. Let children experience a multitude of nonalcohol-related activities. This gives the message you can have lots of fun without using alcohol or other drugs.

Children like vacations, fancy bikes, and other luxuries, but what they really want and need is your time. Spend time with your child. Take walks, read, have picnics. Show him affection. Give hugs and kisses and winks.

Talk with your child about the dangers of alcohol and other drug use.

Accentuate the positive.

Counter media and peer messages with facts.

Set a good example.

Ultimately the decision to use or not to use alcohol and other drugs is the child's. Parents can't control and can't cure their children's drug or alcohol problems. Despite the best intentions and parental support, some children will become involved with alcohol or other drugs. If this happens, seek help.

Juvenile Delinquency

First let us develop a frame of reference. There are two types of juvenile offenses: criminal offenses, which would be crimes for an adult (e.g., shoplifting), and status offenses, which are illegal because of age (e.g., truancy and underage drinking). The definition of a juvenile varies from state to state. A juvenile is a person not yet considered a legal adult.

In thirty-eight states, juveniles are under eighteen. In four states, they are fourteen or younger. In eight states, juveniles are children under seventeen.

Most juveniles start and stay with minor status and/or property offenses. Six percent of the entire juvenile population commit a major property or personal offense, with one half of those committing a second offense. These numbers are not tremendous. But if your child is part of that percentage, it can be devastating. Parents wonder where they went wrong. They are afraid of what is going to happen to their child. They are mad at their child for doing something so "dumb." When they ask why, children often answer honestly, "I don't know." When you want answers and want them now, "I don't know" just doesn't seem adequate.

Often kids' impulsive behavior gets them into trouble and they don't know why. They pick up a rock to throw it at a wasp nest and a window gets broken. They shoot BBs at a sidewalk, and they ricochet off the street and damage someone's property. They do not stop and think about consequences. Kids are shocked. Steve Erkel of television's *Family Matters* plays this type of role perfectly. He breaks something or sends a rocket through the roof of the house and asks, "Did I do that?"

Things happen. Kids would do anything to take back the action. Parents are dumbfounded. Police show up at the door. One more thing gone wrong. How did their kid get into this spot? He did not stop and think.

Most children with ADD don't make successful criminals. They are usually very open, and since most acts are not planned, they get caught. That is not much comfort to parents, but it is important to remember.

Lack of social skills makes children with ADD susceptible to negative peer influences. They often are not good at analyzing situations and predicting that something bad will happen. They often tag along with friends, never believing they will get into trouble. This lack of social intuition may also place a child at risk for victimization. He may speak out, not realizing he is offending others, and find himself in a risky situation.

Such children do not seem to understand the concept of guilt by association. They reason that if they aren't doing anything they shouldn't get into trouble. For instance, Billy drove an acquaintance to a friend's house to pick up football tickets. This gesture of friendship seemed pretty innocent. How could something so simple get a child into trouble? The problem was that no one was home, and his acquaintance was "breaking and entering" as the Billy sat in the car. "I wasn't doing anything and didn't know what he was doing," he proclaimed as the police arrived. Kids with ADD seem to have a knack for being in the wrong place at the wrong time. You may say that they should know better, but the impulsivity of the disorder gets in the way of clear thinking and understanding.

Again, not all children with ADD will become delinquents or even become involved with the police. Some are at higher risk than others. Children who are diagnosed with ADD at a later age, or who do not receive proper management of their symptoms, may suffer more problems because they have not learned to manage their impulsive behaviors.

How impulsivity is manifested changes as the child matures. In the early grades children may rush through worksheets. In adolescence they may drive through stop signs or act hastily in addition to rushing through school work. If impulsivity results in academic and social problems, the child may be at higher risk for delinquency.

What comes first? Do children get into trouble because they can't do well in school or socially? Or do they do poorly in school because they are acting out impulsive behaviors? Regardless of which you feel is the antecedent event, the link between poor academic performance and delinquency cannot be denied. Children who are delinquent often have educational handicaps; some achieve years behind their cohorts and drop out of school. Low academic skills, especially verbal skills, low social skills, and the child's low expectation of achievement in school are often part of the profile of delinquent children.

In the book *Adolescents at Risk,* author Joy G. Dryfoos identifies the following as antecedents to delinquency:

- Low academic expectations.
- Low achievement in school.
- Low participation in school activities.
- Misbehavior.
- Conduct problems, stealing, truancy, lying.
- Early substance use.

- Aggressive behavior/hyperactivity/anxiety.
- Families involved in high-risk behavior.
- Families with extreme parenting styles.

This list does not include every factor that could precede delinquency, but it does shine some light on how children with ADD could be at risk.

What works to prevent delinquency

Early intervention is one idea whose worth has been proven over and over again. Start young, build skills, teach compensating or by-pass strategies, and you will have provided some protection against future problems.

Parenting programs also help. Studies indicate that very authoritarian or very submissive parents can be a problem. This is difficult, because parents of impulsive or hyperactive children have a tendency to be superstrict as a reaction to their child's behavior. Parents may feel they are protecting their kids. The truth is, kids need guidance, not a dictator. We aren't saying kids don't need discipline or structure. But parents who adopt a "My way or the highway" style of parenting will find they might be creating more problems than they solve. This might work in early childhood, but it never teaches kids how to make their own decisions.

Parenting children with ADD can be stressful. If you find yourself lowering the boom more than you'd like, consider taking a parenting class. Often we are so close to the issues that we need some distance to get a perspective. Parenting classes can help us take an objective look at our parenting style and make any necessary changes.

Schools can be a big help in preventing delinquency. Proactive teaching and cooperative learning and helps each child feel he is a valued and valuable member of the class and increases competency and confidence. Prevention programs such as Quest, which fosters moral reasoning and problem-solving, help children develop the skills and competencies they need to lower their risk.

The atmosphere in many communities toward school misbehavior is becoming one of punishment. Despite the widely held belief that this is what kids need, research indicates otherwise. School practices found not effective in changing misbehavior were suspension, detention, expulsion, security guards, and corporal punishment.

What doesn't work

The list goes on. Number one is pharmacological intervention. Medications have their place, but using them alone, without managing symptoms, is asking for trouble. The best prevention is to build skills and confidence. A pill can give you a window of opportunity, but it can't teach a child to solve problems, and it can't give a child confidence or prevent delinquency.

Probation offices, "scaring straight," and other court interventions also have not been shown to *prevent* delinquency, although they may be helpful in intervening in an existing problem.

This information presents a dilemma for parents. Parents are often advised to involve the court system if they have a problem with noncompliance. The idea is that once kids have had a taste of the system, they will be more responsive to parents and more aware of the consequences of their actions. We know of cases where this worked. For some children, just the promise of legal intervention can be a deterrent. Obviously this can only work when the child knows parents always follow through with a promise. The problem here is that one indicator of continual delinquency is early involvement with the legal system. Some kids seem to feel they need to live up to our low expectations. Their negative behavior may be reinforced by involvement with courts and association with peers who have committed serious offenses. It's a hard one to call.

It's always easier to prevent a problem than it is to fix or change behavior after it has become established. Keeping that in mind we are including a table from the U.S. Department of Health and Human Services publication *Preventing Adolescent Drug Use* showing both risk and protective factors.

Just as we discovered our child's strengths in the beginning of this

Figure 8-1
Adolescent Drug Use: Risk and Protective Factors

RISK FACTORS

INDIVIDUAL FACTORS
- A history of personality problems, especially those related to aggression, impulsivity, or depression.
- School failure and academic difficulties, especially if they have resulted in grade retention.
- Involvement in other problem behaviors, including precocious sexual activity, truancy, or non-drug-related criminal or delinquent behavior.

INTERPERSONAL FACTORS
- Distant or hostile relations with parents or guardians.
- Familial disruptions, reconstitution, and martial conflict.
- Membership in a peer group that encourages or tolerates alcohol and drug use.

INSTITUTIONAL FACTORS
- School transition that involves movement in a more impersonal, more anonymous, and less protected environment.
- Involvement in the part-time labor force in excess of 20 hours per week.
- Lack of access to meaningful roles in the community.
- Growing up in poverty.

PROTECTIVE FACTORS

INDIVIDUAL FACTORS
- Academic success.
- A sense of self-efficacy and personal responsibility.
- Well-developed social and interpersonal skills.
- Adequate decision-making skills and intellectual abilities.

INTERPERSONAL FACTORS
- Having at least one close relationship with a parent, teacher, relative, or mentor who can provide both guidance and emotional support.
- Membership in a peer group that actively discourages alcohol and drug use and encourages academic, athletic, or artistic accomplishments as routes to popularity and status.

INSTITUTIONAL
- A sense of bonding to school and other societal institutions.
- An acceptance of societally approved values and expectations for behavior.

book, we can uncover our own strengths too. We can use our strengths and energy to implement many of these protective factors.

We can help our children develop a sense of self-efficacy and responsibility. We can help them develop social and interpersonal skills. These can be accomplished by role modeling, or practicing with our children.

It seems we keep coming back to unconditional positive regard. We keep coming back to that one person who provides emotional support and guidance.

Family Coping Styles

The child's struggle for autonomy, developmental issues, social concerns, worries about the child's future—these all cause stress and concern for family members. In an effort to cope, the family of a child with ADD might begin to function similar to families with an alcoholic or chemically dependent member.

The family may start focusing on the individual with ADD and all the related life problems. They might unintentionally develop roles that enable the child, teen, or adult to continue with problematic behaviors instead of developing coping skills.

This is done out of love and out of a need to maintain some sort of stability in the home. Healthy families thrive on consistency and stability; unfortunately these are rare commodities in the homes of individuals with ADD.

All this talk about substance use, school failure, and delinquency is not meant to give you another worry as parents. It is meant to give you something to think about and talk about.

Families with substance abuse often adopt a "Don't talk, don't tell" policy. If you see a problem in your family, talk about it. Tell your child what you think and feel. Find a safe support system to get you through the difficult times.

Sam Goldstein, Ph.D., of Neurology Learning Behavior Center in Salt Lake City, Utah, reports that more than medications, therapy, or educational intervention, the best predictors of a successful outcome are:

- Parents' acceptance of the adolescent with ADD.
- Development of a close, positive relationship.
- Patient and persistent dealing with school and community resources.
- Providing critical insulation around child.
- Parents who are proud of child.

Tag-team parents

Bill and Ruth Guentter have come up with a creative survival technique for parenting their children with ADD. They call it tag-team parenting. When one parent has reached his or her capacity, the other carries the ball for a while. "It's the only way we survive," Ruth said. "If one parent needs to drop out and rejuvenate for a while, it's OK."

If you are a single parent, find a friend or relative with whom you can team up. Maybe one parent will carry a bigger part of the burden. What really matters is that you provide that insulation from criticism and failure around your child.

Again, knowing your own strengths makes management easier. Nick has never mastered talking to teachers in a tactful way or using "I" statements. We don't send him to conferences or let him talk to teachers on the phone. On the other hand, he's a whiz at math and is great at teaching the kids life skills like cutting grass, working on cars, and changing oil. He likes the outdoors and likes spending the day with the guys, fishing or camping. He models caring for elderly parents and helping the "mechanically impaired" keep their lawn mowers running. Nick keeps the sports equipment organized and the kids on schedule.

Darlene is the reader, talks to the teachers, advocates for services, goes to IEP meetings, and helps with term papers or book reports. She's in charge of trips to the library and is the recording secretary when the kids are doing research.

In Nancy's household, David is the voice of reason. At teacher conferences, he remains calm and rational and can internalize what is being said. He listens carefully, weighs the information, then gives a response. Around the house, he is Mr. Fix-It. He is our storyteller and song leader (even though he only knows the first line of every song). He always sees the bright side of life, and his humor has defused many tense situations. His organizational system consists of piles on the floor or table and his daily planner. He models the values of a strong work ethic, honesty, and integrity.

Nancy is the glue that maintains her family's structure. She uses lists and charts and calendars to provide consistency and routine. By juggling everyone's schedule, she keeps the household running smoothly. She oversees the fulfillment of responsibilities and monitors school progress. To avoid power struggles, Nancy gives choices and sets boundaries. She is the drafter of contracts for everything from driving privileges to going to college. Both she and David are strong problem solvers and present a united front.

Each parent maximizes the results by doing what comes naturally for them. They use their strengths. Why swim against the current if you can swim with it? Get the balance sheet from the beginning of the book and identify your strengths. Use the symptoms side to identify your deficits. Be honest. If you are impatient, you probably don't want to spend an afternoon looking through card catalog at the library. You can model the strengths perspective, teach your child some valuable life lessons, and make your own life easier in the process.

You will find that, depending on how the parents' strengths and difficulties match those of the child, one parent may end up handling a larger burden of responsibility for assisting the child with ADD. This can be discouraging, and one parent may feel used and abused. It's important to remember that helping your child isn't about what is fair and equal. What each parent, teacher, and professional gives a child will depend on his or her own strengths and abilities. If one parent has ADD or is hyperactive or impulsive, he may find it difficult to assist with bypass strategies.

What the parent who shares the symptoms with the child can do is to encourage. You've been there and done that. Your encouragement can keep the child going. Share your difficult times with your child and motivate him to keep trying. Share how you overcame obstacles, and be a model of what can be achieved.

9

Accentuating the Positive

In the 1940s, Johnny Mercer wrote a song with the above title. It was good advice then and even better advice today. Let's not fool ourselves. Life with children with ADD will have its downs. At times we will feel like we are going crazy. We'll be angry, our feelings will be hurt, we will be afraid, and we'll have a few good cries. It's OK to be there. It's not OK to be stuck there. How we think about things affects how we feel, and how we feel affects how we act. Huh, you say?

Let's say we are thinking our kids will never pass second grade. We believe they are going to be failures, and if they fail they will never go to college, never get a job, and never be able to live on their own. These thoughts make us feel pretty low. The more we think about their miserable future, the more depressed we become. The more depressed or down we feel the more we isolate ourselves from support systems, such as family, friends, and groups. We may be angry at the school and angry at our kids because they are going to live at home forever. We might yell at our children for every little thing that goes wrong. We start to yell at our spouse because if he or she helped more, our children would not be headed for a future of failure. Pretty silly, you say? It's surprising how quickly we can get sidetracked by negative thoughts.

Just suppose that same child is having trouble in second grade and we think we need to get some extra help for him in math. We believe that doing this will help him learn a skill. We believe teachers, seeing how committed we are to helping our child, will go out of their way to help our child as well, and our child can be successful. We acknowledge that if this isn't completely successful we can send our child to summer school or get summer tutoring so he will be up to par and ready for the third grade. All these things are pretty positive. Believing all these things will help put us in a good mood. We might thank teachers for any extra efforts and we might continually compliment our child on the effort he is showing and accentuate each new skill learned. We might even smile at our spouse. Our spouse might take us out to dinner.

These examples are probably a little extreme, but they illustrate what a difference in feelings and outcome there is between accentuating the negative and accentuating the positive. We don't know about anyone else, but we are kind of partial to good thoughts, good feelings, and good news.

Keep a Smile on Your Face and a Song in Your Heart

We said in the beginning, life with children with ADD is never boring. Parents have a choice. Develop a sense of humor or live in the swamp of despair. Believe us, choose a sense of humor and you will have chosen wisely. Children with ADD seem to have an inordinate amount of curiosity and a knack for experimentation. Just remember, Thomas Edison once blew up his lab, and he turned out OK. We are not advocating letting children experiment with dangerous chemicals, but we should recognize and encourage this curiosity. You never know what you might learn. Don't ask why they do it. It's like the mountain— they do these things because they are there, and maybe because they have ADD. These traits which so often drive people crazy might be the very traits that lead to amazing discoveries, works of art, and satisfying lives.

Things you'd never know if you didn't have a child with ADD:

1. Effervescent tablets are also good for cleaning the toilet bowl.
2. Toothbrushes don't flush, they float in the trap.
3. Charcoal dust mixed with water makes excellent paint.
4. Tennis shoes don't leak pancake syrup.
5. A child can do a 360-degree flip on a bike and not get hurt.
6. You can't stop overflowing toilets with towels.
7. Overflowing toilets will short out telephone lines and electric stoves.
8. Put a sled on a skateboard and you'll crash every time you go down the hill.
9. It is possible to estimate the number of stitches it takes to sew a gash with absolute accuracy.
10. It is possible to bend a bike rim by jumping over homemade three-foot ramps.
11. Plungers belong in toy boxes.
12. Twenty-five baby water snakes will comfortably fit in a two-liter soda bottle.
13. If you click "Delete all" in file manager you will delete everything from your computer's hard drive.
14. It is possible to write your name in the lawn with a riding mower.
15. Peanut-butter bread will stick to ceilings.
16. It is possible to lose homework between the school front door and your homeroom desk.
17. Baby birds eat softened dog food.
18. It is possible to do all your homework in the school cafeteria and on the school bus.

19. No matter how many eggs you crack open on the living room rug, they will all have the yellow things in the middle of them.

Warning: These learning opportunities have been provided by experts and should not be tried at home.

You might notice that many of these delightful learning experiences involve toilets. We are not sure why. If your child with ADD is in the bathroom and silent for any length of time, we advise investigation.

Keeping a song in your heart might also help you keep that sense of humor. A little zany behavior never hurt anyone. Jimmy's mom changed the lyrics "Shimmy, Shimmy, Coco Puff" to "Jimmy, Jimmy, Coco Puff" and then chased him around the room, trying to catch him so she could eat him up. Parents need to have fun too. Anything that focuses on the positive and lightens the mood should be encouraged.

Music can provide an avenue for positive messages. Younger children will respond to songs like *I Love You a Bushel and a Peck* or *This Little Light of Mine*. Older children might want something more contemporary. Find a love song for your family. When it comes on the radio, get up and jump around or hug each other. Take every opportunity to have fun with your children. They have so much exuberance and they need someone to model a healthy way of displaying it.

Living Happily Ever After

ADD can be an asset in the real world, where many of the behaviors or symptoms causing children so much trouble in school aren't a problem. Distractibility and the free flow of ideas can be used to discover creative solutions to problems. Individuals with ADD aren't restricted by the current story or the way things are. They are constantly looking for new ways or investigating what-ifs. These qualities might not be valued in the classroom, but corporate America values a problem solver. In the real world, qualities that can't be quantified, like the ability to work with other people and overcome obstacles, are an asset.

We've said it before and we'll say it again. Success in school doesn't necessarily equate with success in adult life, and neither does failure.

Baskets and Dave Longaberger

Dave Longaberger wasn't very successful in the classroom. Epilepsy, severe stuttering, two years in first grade and three in the fifth grade might destroy the will of most people. But Dave found a way to detour around the disabilities that hampered his success in school.

What he lacked in academic skills, Dave made up for with a strong work ethic and people skills. Dave got his first job at a neighborhood grocery store when he was seven years old. It seems Dave had an abundance of energy. As a youngster, he was already busy working in the grocery business and at cutting grass, shoveling snow, and delivering papers.

Dave worked hard and dreamed big. But even his dreams weren't as big as his eventual success. In the book *The Longaberger Story,* coauthored with Steve Williford, he recalls high school graduation.

"Finally I graduated from high school! I was very insecure. I wasn't taking myself too seriously. My self-esteem was very low. Because what could I do? I was only reading at a fifth- or sixth-grade level. How was a dumb kid like myself going to go anywhere in life?"

Go somewhere he did. Today he is the CEO of a $100 million a year business and the winner of the Vision for Tomorrow Award from the Direct Selling Association, an award presented to a company that has substantially improved the quality of life for its community.

Success did not come easily or quickly. Still, Dave never let his handicaps or roadblocks deter him for long.

"Most handicaps are not permanent roadblocks. If the fifth oldest boy of twelve children, who flunked three times in elementary school, who stuttered so bad people could barely understand him, who couldn't secure a loan from the bank to save his life, can reach his goals, so can you! Regardless of your circumstances, background, or abilities, you can be successful, if you are willing to do what it takes."

Dave still has traits that many would consider roadblocks to success. "He still can't sit still for very long, and he still loves change. The common joke is: Put your desk on rollers, because you'll soon be in a different office—or building—or town." He has overcome adversity and roadblocks by believing in himself, working hard, and loving what he does.

Overcoming adversity

Specialization is a way many children with ADD overcome adversity. Children with ADD become experts in adversity. They have lots of opportunity to practice problem solving and discover new or different ways to survive. When you work hard to achieve, you learn lots of ways of approaching problems. The positive side is that the struggles of a child with ADD can help him relate to others' struggles—a wonderful plus in the real world.

Adulthood allows and encourages specialization. During school years, especially elementary school, students are expected to be good at everything. The farther a student goes in school, the more opportunity for specialization.

Darlene's son Tim will never be an English major. But he has great analytical and math abilities. Now a senior, he is able to concentrate on classes in his strengths, such as physics, mechanical drawing, calculus, and computer programming. These help him develop a skill set that is very marketable. He can further develop these skills in post–highschool studies.

The key to success for kids with ADD is finding something they enjoy and are good at and building on it. When allowed to do that, they grow. If something is purposeful and has meaning, it is easier to master. As an adult, your child will be able to work in an area he is excited about, one that is rewarding for him, and hopefully he will be fairly compensated. For this reason, children with ADD often make much more successful adults than elementary students.

Pen chewers

Tom's teacher crossed her arms and shook her head. "I just don't know what to do with him. He's always got something in his mouth. He chews on pens. He plays with paper clips," she said. Another teacher added, "He'll never get along in the real world with these behaviors."

They didn't know Rick Leffler. Rick, 40, is the manager of application development for the Polk Company in Cincinnati. Rick oversees all new systems development. Rick Leffler is a pen chewer.

Pen chewing is a physical expression of Leffler's mental energy. "I began chewing on pens in high school or junior high," reports Leffler. "It releases energy and allows me to concentrate. When lots of ideas are going in at the same time, when I am listening to others' ideas, taking that information in, forming my own ideas, and storing and compartmentalizing that information, chewing on a pen helps channel that energy. With all the mental energy required to handle all these ideas, it's like static accumulating. If you can't get rid of the extra energy, ideas get short-circuited," Leffler said.

"Pen chewing is not distracting in any way from my thought process. It has become part of my thought process. I associate chewing on a pen with thinking." He acknowledges his pen chewing may distract others, but feels lucky to be surrounded by people who tolerate it and who have strengths that compensate for his weakness.

Rick has never been diagnosed with ADD and doesn't feel it matters. "There is too much focus on fixing and not enough tolerance for differences. Is a label as important as an awareness of skills, competencies . . . as tolerance by others?" he asks.

"Let kids know it is OK to fail and OK not to know," he advises parents. "Make the best of what you have . . . don't worry about what you don't have."

"Sometimes those who don't struggle may be very smart. But they're independent, thinking, 'I can do it all'. The only good idea is their idea. They may be intelligent but have no social skills or not be able to work with others," says Leffler.

"I still have concentration problems . . . good days and bad days

. . . if bored or working outside of what is interesting (what I think is boring, not what others find boring). Sometimes I'm not satisfied with the quality of my work or output even though others, my superiors, are. I will keep working until I'm satisfied, and when everything is satisfying, it becomes boring and I need a change. I need challenges."

Leffler advises children to acknowledge their limits and then make choices about them: You can decide to live within your limits. You can decide to overcome your limits. And if you want to overcome, you can decide if it's worth the price you will have to pay.

Our kids can probably do anything. Sometimes it might not be worth the price. When and if we decide the cost of achievement is too high, we can decide to pursue other things. But the choice is ours. It doesn't appear that being a pen chewer is a sentence to failure, does it?

It helps to discover others in our community who have walked in our shoes, or those who have struggled with difficulties and overcome them. These people can be an inspiration and a valuable source of information to both parents and children.

Letters to Parents

We have included messages from several parents we have been fortunate to know. All of these parents have learned to use their strengths. They have been unrelenting in their quest for information. They have educated their school and advocated for their children, often against great odds. They have enriched our lives and made a difference for all children who march to the beat of a different drummer. They are truly inspirational.

The last letter in this section is from a young man. His words eloquently provide proof that the struggle to parent a child with ADD is worthwhile and can be very rewarding.

Don't give up

When you feel something is wrong with your child and doctors don't see it, go with your feeling and keep searching until you find a doctor who understands all the problems your child might have. A mother knows the child better than others. Sometimes you might be able to identify or relate because you might discover you have the same problems as your child.

Sometimes you have to be a detective and follow through with clues. You might be accused of doctor hopping, trying to find some-one who agrees with your ideas. There are times when one physician can't diagnose all the problems some children will have. You wind up all pieces of the pie. You get a little information here and there. You need someone to put them together. You may need to go to several who are specialists in each area that is a problem for your child. Most children won't have as many difficulties as my child. But if you aren't satisfied with the answers you are getting, keep looking.

When my son was three and a half, doctors thought he was mentally ill. He didn't talk when he was supposed to. He wouldn't sleep; he was always fidgeting and acting out. He was finally diagnosed as having attention deficit hyperactivity disorder when he was six years old.

The doctors thought that was his only problem until fifth grade. He was taking Ritalin but was still not improving. He couldn't write well, couldn't read. I started reading articles and began to suspect learning disabilities. During the sixth grade, he did great. He was taught the way he learned. His grades and self-esteem improved. When he got to the seventh and eighth grade, the school took the intervention away and behavior came out everywhere. Behavior got worse.

The school wanted to place him in a severe behavior handicapped class. When we had our child evaluated by a psychiatrist, we discovered he had Tourette's with facial tics.

As long as our child had a good teacher who believed in him, things were OK. When we had teachers who didn't believe he had learning disabilities—because he appeared so bright or they couldn't believe one child could have so many problems and assumed he wasn't trying—he fell apart.

I have had to fight the school all along. It has been frustrating and stressful. They think you are babying your child or making excuses. I knew from reading and watching him I was right. I just couldn't find the help he needed.

Finally my son was tutored one on one. It was the tutor who realized he could not learn in the conventional way, and she became his advocate. She developed interventions so he could learn. I often wonder where he would be today if he had gotten the understanding and interventions he needed when he was young.

There were many times when I felt tired and frustrated. All you can do is regroup, gather strength, and go on trying to help others to understand that your child can't do it and is not choosing not to.

I also have a learning disability. I have difficulty with expressive language. I have often been frustrated by my own inability to communicate what I want to say. In spite of my disabilities, I have tried to always advocate for my son and educate those who will listen.

So preserve and keep educating yourself. Don't think because you have a disability you can't do it. Read, learn, and keep trying.

—Judy Leonard-Case

What mama never told me, or the nitty-gritty of being a parent of a child with ADHD

Years ago I read an article about living with "difficult" children, and the author said that the hardest part was being the parent you had to be (always firm, consistent, etc.) instead of the parent you wanted to be (lenient, easygoing, fun). It's not that I have trouble as a parent being consistent (boy, can I be consistent) or setting limits or goals or negotiating or giving time-outs or making charts or manipulating the environment to encourage success. We didn't expect parenting to be a piece of cake—we knew it would be challenging at times. It's just that we didn't anticipate that the times go on forever. Our pediatricians in the early years of our son's life told us he was just going through a stage, but they forgot to tell us it was a stage that lasts a lifetime!

As a new mom at the YMCA infant gym class, I wondered why my child didn't enjoy it and all the others did. Other mothers looked forward to picking their children up from nursery school, seeing what artistic creation they'd made for Mommy. I cringed as I went in to hear the usual tales from the teachers about various out-of-control escapades my son had been up to that day. Others parents beamed proudly at the kindergarten music recital. We clenched our jaws. While little Ignatius sang a solo in Filipino and played the violin, our son refused to sing, played with his shoelaces, picked his nose, and started a squabble with the child sitting next to him. Perhaps he had allergies, one well-meaning teacher suggested. "He's just all boy!" said another. One even said he was hyperactive because he ate pancakes too often for breakfast! (As the humorist Dave Barry says: No, I am not making this up.) Another teacher said he was "immature" and should be held back—advice we thankfully did not take. My sister said the problem was that I was too strict. My brother-in-law encouraged us to be firm. My mother said she didn't see a problem—we must be imagining it. My mother-in-law claimed we must be purposefully turning our son against her because he was so obnoxious with her. I was very thankful for my husband, who, just as frustrated and bewildered as I was, knew it wasn't our fault and that it wasn't a "stage" and that it wasn't pancakes, and couldn't have cared less what our relatives thought.

Well-intentioned but unhelpful parenting columns and talk shows suggested we take time to laugh or smile and look at the humorous side. What humorous side? we wondered. "Take time out to be by yourselves," these experts said, but they weren't offering to baby-sit for us, and nobody else wanted to!

There was a great deal of relief when our son was finally diagnosed at the end of first grade with AD/HD. He tested at a very high IQ and was described by his psychologist as "a child of superior intellectual capacity." We were very concerned, as are almost all parents, about putting our child on psycho-stimulant medication. But his response to the medication was dramatic. His teachers called him a changed person, now able to fulfill his obvious potential. There was a sense that this problem could be dealt with, if not conquered. Our son's second-grade teacher understood ADHD and was supportive and enthusiastic about helping him. I became involved with the ADD Council, which provided an enormous amount of information and support for us.

Our son's doctor had recommended "drug holidays" on weekends and vacations, and it made sense to us that the least possible medication would be best. Except that nothing much improved at home! Extracurricular sports were still a nightmare, play dates were nerve-racking, we were exhausted, and we still seemed to be doing way too much nagging. "He needs time to just be himself," we were told. There was very little sympathy for us, the parents. So we read a lot of books, talked to a lot of professionals in the field, and found a psychiatrist experienced in working with children with ADHD. Now, with a lot more knowledge under our belts and a little trial-and-error at finding out what works best, we medicate on weekends and vacations as well. This provides us with some time with our son when we aren't constantly having to monitor and criticize his behavior.

He can get himself up and dressed in under an hour about 75 percent of the time now. He can actually participate in sports activity and experiences some success. He can have a friend over and maintain some semblance of self-control. Other children don't describe him as "wild" or "weird." He can go for several hours without fighting with his little brothers. He's having a lot more fun, and so are we. Things are not perfect, of course. Some days are better than others, and we could use some time off occasionally. My sister-in-law still calls our son "high care" and our relatives still don't offer to baby-sit, but we manage somehow.

Knowledge is power, the old saying goes. Knowledge about ADHD can make you informed and assertive parents. It can also help parents maintain their balance and their sanity. Reading every book on the subject and experimenting with different management techniques helps. Attending support-group meetings and talking with others who have been there helps tremendously. Listening to others can put your own problem in perspective, as there is always someone who has a more overwhelming task at home. But together we can find ways to cope. So, I guess parenting turned out to be a lot more challenging than anyone warned us. Now we are beginning to realize we really can meet that challenge.

—Kay Colbert

ADD teen and the steering wheel

When your teen comes to you at the age of fifteen and asks about a driver's license, fear comes to mind. Don't panic; have faith in your teen. Accidents, tickets, and high insurance rates may be what you think of. These are concerns you can work through. Remember that after your child turns eighteen, your permission isn't needed. Wouldn't it be better to work with your teen, to do it the right way, than have him or her go to a stranger who has no knowledge of the situation? I had enough faith in my son and worked out a plan with him. I didn't hold my son back because I didn't trust him. I used the license as a positive tool to advance my son to adulthood.

I was nervous at the beginning, but I set rules on how we were going to bring this important part of my son's life to a positive end. Listed below are ways I handled the situation.

1. I sat my son down and we did everything as a team. I didn't do anything behind his back. Everything I did we talked about first.
2. I contacted his doctor for his opinion and input.
3. I met with the school psychologist to work out goals to advance through the process.
4. The first goals were to get a learner's permit and obtain permission to sign up for driver's education. My son needed a C average with no failing grades for the semester he was in. (If it is too late to get the grades up for the current semester, then use the next full semester.)
5. When your teen earns his learner's permit, don't just turn him over to a driving school. Get involved. Then take him out and

teach him. You are going to be nervous at first, but if you do it right, it will wear off fast. Don't start out in rush-hour traffic. Start by going forward and backward in your driveway. Next, move to a parking lot to learn to control the car. When you feel comfortable, start using the streets with light traffic. From that point, just take it a step at a time. Remember, he will be getting help from driver's education also. Talk to the instructor and get his feedback on how your teen is progressing.

6. The proudest moment is when your teen is ready and goes for the test and walks out with the license. If he fails the first time, talk with the inspector to find out the problem. *Don't yell and scream.* Work on solving the problem.

7. Don't turn over the keys right away. At first, when he drives, a parent must be in the car. When you feel comfortable, start with a solo drive on a weekend, in daylight, and proceed from there.

This may sound like a big job. It is. It took me six months after my son got his license to give him full responsibility to drive with no restrictions. The most important requirement is that he must maintain a B average to keep driving. Remember, at this point you don't have to run a taxi service anymore, and you will have someone to do your running. Good Luck!

—Frank Monaco

Reach out

In 1988 I was given Judy Leonard-Case's phone number as my son was being diagnosed with ADD. She shared with me her knowledge of this disorder as well as names of area doctors who might help my son. I began attending meetings of the local support group and found the information and fellowship very rewarding. I encouraged my husband, Bill, to attend, and we eventually took on various jobs within the group.

Thinking about how I got involved with this group reminded me that the sharing with other parents in similar situations was as important for me as the speakers at the meetings. And this is exactly what I believed would be helpful to many of the parents and adults with ADD that come to our meetings every month. People need to be sharing with each other and exchanging phone numbers and getting together outside of the meetings to provide support for each other. We are all qualified to do this and can learn from each other. Those in our group are just a bunch of volunteers trying to fill a need—we aren't specialized professionals. I am a mom with no special college degrees, and our group includes a receptionist, a meat cutter, a carpenter, a truck driver. What we have in common is the desire to change attitudes and educate the community and make the world a better and more understanding place for our children. We can provide the basic tools and reach out to the community, but it is up to others—to you—to reach out to the community and change it.

One way you can do this is by starting your own support group, perhaps in your school. Parents find it very helpful to share information and coping strategies with each other. In addition, each school is different, and it only makes sense for those who have common goals and situations to work together. It can be a lifesaver to talk with people who are going through the same things you are and who don't look at you strangely when you describe your kids' antics! Your doctor isn't always available, and often doctors don't understand firsthand the dynamics of a family with ADD.

It is also important to build a rapport with others in the same situation. Approach your principal tactfully with the idea, and let him or her know that you will not be a threat but rather a means to help parents. In addition, you can serve as a resource for teachers. Your group could meet for a set period and have a short-term goal. You might meet once a month only during the school year to share information or to organize an in-service for teachers. There could be a topic for discussion each time, such as diagnosis, medication, coping skills, home strategies, etc. School nurses, counselors, or special education teachers all could assist with communicating with parents about your group.

I am very familiar with the demands of a busy schedule, but you have to make the time. It is sometimes hard for me to make arrangements to attend monthly meetings, and I would go in dragging. But I always felt better after hearing other people's stories and suggestions. Good luck!

—Ruth Guentter

A letter to my parents as written by a child with ADD

Dear Mom and Dad,

Well, you're finished raising me now that I am, at last, a grown man preparing to graduate from college. I am old enough to take care of all the responsibilities I have been promised, and the first of these is to thank you. You above all have been patient through all the accidents, detentions, suspensions, principal/teacher visits, "white lies," and other eccentricities. You should be praised for seeing my true self all the while others, as well as myself, discounted me as a lost cause.

Thank you for being firm and not allowing me to make excuses for my behavior or use my ADD as an excuse. As bitter a pill as this lesson was to swallow, I now thrive. I know I have to take responsibility for all my actions, not just the positive ones.

Thank you for the tireless hours of helping me with my homework, reports, and the like. All those organizational strategies did help. Thank you for sending me to tutors when my pre-calculus grade was in the single digits. Thank you for backing me up when I faced surly and ignorant administrators.

But most of all, thank you for being my parents. I know that I could never have picked them, but if there is an award, you deserve it. No one else I know has ever felt the pain that I felt like you did. I never could figure out why you cried when I got into trouble, but now I know. You felt my pain, my fear, and my disappointment. You knew, through me, what it was like to constantly be knocked down and how difficult it was for me to catch a break. I now know that you didn't cry because you thought what I did was stupid, but you knew the potential that I am just realizing. Thank you for never giving up. I know I have made you proud, and I am glad I was given that chance.

Gratefully,
Your son,
Christian

Epilogue

Whirlwinds

As parents we may be overwhelmed and even intimidated by those we consider to have authority positions in our children's school or in our community. Meetings with teachers or principals may make you quiver and reach for the Maalox tablets. We all have the strength and can get the knowledge to meet these challenges head on. From this book you have learned what ADD is and how it is manifested in your child. You understand your child's strengths and learning style. You know how to communicate with professionals, how to have a parent-teacher conference and to problem solve. You have more skills and knowledge about your child than many professionals do! Remind yourself that you are a multitalented person. You have strengths. Often we are unaware of these talents until called upon to use them. The following story illustrates the possibilities.

There is a great people called the whirlwinds. These people possess many strengths and were known throughout the neighboring nations as creative, joyful people. Their unique way of looking at life and problems has long been admired, and they are responsible for many new inventions and beautiful creations.

Under the loving care of their elders, the young whirlwinds grow strong in a nation where each person is valued.

One young girl became a woman, married, and had a beautiful young whirlwind son who was loved and cherished by her nation. After much time the family moved from their homeland to the nation of Anyschl.

The elders of the Anyschl believed they had "the truth" (the only truth). They watched the young whirlwind whirl and dance and said "That is not our way." But the young whirlwind would not be stilled. He flittered and fluttered from place to place. His dance was one of enthusiasm. But the Anyschl elders were angered by the dance. "The young whirlwind does not honor our ways," they cried. "The whirl-wind ways are destructive and dangerous. If we let him dance this dance of his, others will not listen to our ways—they will stray from the one true way."

It was decided that if the young whirlwind would not obey the Anyschl elders, he would be punished. The elders banned the young whirlwind from speaking with others of the Anyschl youth, and he was shut in a great cave, whose entrance was then barred by a huge boulder.

The young whirlwind was afraid and confused. Had not his elders taught him being a whirlwind was good? Why then did these others not honor him? Why did they lock him away from their children? What was wrong with him?

Shut in the huge cave and prevented from dancing, he felt his power and joy begin to drain away. This worried his mother and father, and although they protested, the Anyschl elders would not be swayed. Mother and Father did their dance of protest and whirled and whirled, but they alone were not strong enough to move the huge boulder and free their son from his prison.

Soon news of the young whirlwind's trouble spread to the whirl-wind homeland. The young wanted to declare war on the Anyschl nation. But the whirlwind elders journeyed to Anyschl to teach their ways and to ask the Anyschl to honor the ways of the young whirl-wind.

At first the Anyschl elders' ears were shut. The whirlwind elders were patient and persistent. At last they persuaded the Anyschl nation that the young whirlwind's ways were not a danger to them. The Anyschl came to learn tolerance and that watching the young whirl-wind dance could bring joy to their lives, for his dance was free and graceful and joyful.

The young whirlwind was so curious that he asked many questions and learned much. He learned there was a time and place to whirl and a time to be peaceful and gentle. As the Anyschl elders saw his gentleness, they became less afraid of his whirling ways.

The whirlwind elders returned to their homeland but not without teaching the Anyschl people a great lesson about honor and diversity. What a few whirlwinds could not accomplish by whirling, the elders accomplished by sharing their wisdom with the other nation. The two nations became great friends, and every five years gathered to celebrate each other and to share each other's ways, for understanding and honor lead to peace.

As parents you might not feel like much of a whirlwind. But you can no longer say, "I didn't know." Let this story remind you that you do have strength and can bring about change. By joining with other parents, you can change even the biggest systems.

It is important to remember the whirlwinds. In the story, being a whirlwind was an asset. It helped solve problems and gave the family the strength to overcome great odds. Like our children, many of us are not aware of our talents; we don't know we too are whirlwinds.

Some segments of society will not value this talent. As we organize and advocate, they will think we are stirring up trouble. We can only hope for the energy to teach them.

Still whirling

Darlene is a big fan of country music. She uses music as conversation starters when facilitating support groups and doing individual counseling, and has developed a reputation for having a country song available for just about any situation. There are many country songs able to inspire parents of children with ADD.

Mary Chapin Carpenter encourages us to look past the pain and trouble by reminding us "there's a whole lot of ground to gain" in the song "Why Walk When You Can Fly." The words of this song remind us of the value of advocating for change and not accepting the status quo. All that we gain through our actions helps not only our children but also those who follow.

Once we have become educated about ADD, it is our responsibility to be like the whirlwind elders and speak out when we observe a lack of equality and fairness. If you need a plan, refer back to the problem-solving chapter to help get you started.

Randy Travis sings a not-so-subtle reminder about how fight talk and "You messages" can hurt and damage those who are on the receiving end of such talk in the song "Small Y'all." Judgmental statements are a big roadblock to success for any person, not just the child with ADD. If we stop and think about how hurtful these messages can be, we may indeed feel small. Like the whirlwind elders we can educate our community and school about the manifestations of ADD and prevent at least some judgmental statements.

There are also messages for our children in the music. These songs validate the uniqueness of our children. The group Blackhawk performs two such songs.

The song "That's Just About Right" advises us that even if you have the greatest intentions, you just got to "do what you do, what you do." You may be searching for the answer—the perfect treatment, education plan, or intervention—when the answer is in the child, in who he is and what his strengths are. In the end, we cannot change who our child is. And why should we? Whether our child's mind whirls into free flight or his emotions or body whirls, he must be who he is and learn to harness his positive qualities.

This group also recorded the song "Let 'em Whirl." It is a wonderful reminder that despite all the skills, strategies, and remediation we provide our children, they still will have ADD, and we must let them be who they are.

Many times judgmental statements will hurt them and knock them down. The damage done to their spirit may send them reeling. They may hesitate to keep trying.

Our job is to let them know it's OK to be who they are. Maybe the school's way or our way isn't the better way, and in the end they will have to decide which way is the best for them. Our kids may learn the hard way, we cannot protect them from hardship. We also can't predict where their journey will take them. We can only give them the tools they need and then let them whirl.

As a final thought about accentuating the positive, we must remember the real value in life isn't in a grade-point average, yearly income, or which college our kids attend. Being right or being number one isn't what matters. The real treasure at the end of the road is the relationships we develop with our children. It is worth repeating. The most significant asset to children with ADD is one person who values them, who is there for them, who supports them. We want to add to that perhaps the most significant asset is also the parent who does all the above and then sets them free and lets them whirl. Who knows where life will lead them!

Appendix A

Diagnostic Criteria for Attention-Deficit/Hyperactivity Disorder

A. Either (1) or (2)

   (1) six (or more) of the following symptoms of inattention have persisted for at least six months to a degree that is maladaptive and inconsistent with developmental level:

Inattention

     (a) often fails to give close attention to details or makes careless mistakes in schoolwork, work, or other activities

     (b) often has difficulty sustaining attention in tasks or play activities

     (c) often does not seem to listen when spoken to directly

     (d) often does not follow through on instructions and fails to finish schoolwork, chores, or duties in the workplace (not due to oppositional behavior or failure to understand instructions)

     (e) often has difficulty organizing tasks and activities

     (f) often avoids, dislikes, or is reluctant to engage in tasks that require sustained mental effort (such as schoolwork or homework)

     (g) often loses things necessary for tasks or activities (e.g., toys, school assignments, pencils, books, or tools)

     (h) is often easily distracted by extraneous stimuli

     (i) is often forgetful in daily activities

   (2) six (or more) of the following symptoms of hyperactivity-impulsivity have persisted for at least six months to a degree that is maladaptive and inconsistent with developmental level:

Hyperactivity

     (a) often fidgets with hands or feet or squirms in seat

    (b) often leaves seat in classroom or in other situations in which remaining seated is expected

    (c) often runs about or climbs excessively in situations in which it is inappropriate (in adolescents or adults, may be limited to subjective feelings of restlessness)

    (d) often has difficulty playing or engaging in leisure activities quietly

    (e) is often "on the go" or often acts as if "driven by a motor"

    (f) often talks excessively

Impulsivity

    (a) often blurts out answers before questions have been completed

    (b) often has difficulty awaiting turn

    (c) often interrupts or intrudes on others (e.g., butts into conversations or games)

B. Some hyperactive-impulsive or inattentive symptoms that caused impairment were present before age seven.

C. Some impairment from the symptoms is present in two or more settings

D. There must be clear evidence of clinically significant impairment in social, academic, or occupational functioning

E. The symptoms do not occur exclusively during the course of a pervasive developmental disorder, schizophrenia, or other psychotic disorder and are not better accounted for by another mental disorder

TYPES:

Attention-Deficit/Hyperactivity Disorder, Combined Type: If both Criterion A1 and Criterion A2 are met for past six months

Attention-Deficit/Hyperactivity Disorder, Predominantly Inattentive Type: If Criterion A1 is met but Criterion A2 is not met for the past six months

Attention-Deficit/Hyperactivity Disorder, Predominantly Hyperactive-Impulsive Type. If Criterion A2 is met but Criterion A1 is not met for the past six months

Appendix B

A. A pattern of negativistic, hostile, and defiant behavior lasting at least six months, during which four (or more) of the following are present:

(1) often loses temper

(2) often argues with adults

(3) often actively defies or refuses to comply with adults' requests or rules

(4) often deliberately annoys people

(5) often blames others for his or her mistakes or misbehavior

(6) is often touchy or easily annoyed by others

(7) is often angry and resentful

(8) is often spiteful and vindictive

Note: Consider a criterion met only if the behavior occurs more frequently than is typically observed in individuals of comparable age and developmental level.

B. The disturbance in behavior causes clinically significant impairment in social, academic, or occupational functioning

C. The behaviors do not occur exclusively during the course of a psychotic or mood disorder

D. Criteria are not met for conduct disorder, and if the individual is age eighteen or older, criteria are not met for antisocial personality disorder

Appendix C

DIAGNOSTIC CRITERIA FOR CONDUCT DISORDER

A. A repetitive and persistent pattern of behavior in which the basic rights of others or major age-appropriate societal norms or rules are violated as manifested by the presences of three (or more) of the following criteria in the past twelve months, with at least one criterion present in the last six months:

Aggression to people and animals
(1) often bullies, threatens, or intimidates others
(2) often initiates physical fights
(3) has used a weapon that can cause serious physical harm to others (e.g., a bat, brick, broken bottle, knife, gun)
(4) has been physically cruel to people
(5) has been physically cruel to animals
(6) has stolen while confronting a victim (e.g., mugging, purse snatching, extortion, armed robbery)
(7) has forced someone into sexual activity

Destruction of property
(8) has deliberately engaged in fire setting with the intention of causing serious damage
(9) has deliberately destroyed others' property (other than by fire setting)

Deceitfulness or theft
(10) has broken into someone else's house, building, or car
(11) often lies to obtain goods or favors or to avoid obligations (i.e., "cons" others)
(12) has stolen items of nontrivial value without confronting a victim (e.g., shoplifting, but without breaking and entering; forgery)

Serious violations of rules

(13) often stays out at night despite parental prohibitions, beginning before age thirteen

(14) has run away from home overnight at least twice while living in parental or parental surrogate home (or once without returning for a lengthy period)

(15) is often truant from school, beginning before age thirteen

B. The disturbance in behavior causes clinically significant impairment in social, academic, or occupational functions

C. If the individual is age eighteen or older, criteria are not met for an antisocial personality disorder

Appendix D

DIAGNOSTIC CRITERIA FOR OBSESSIVE COMPULSIVE DISORDER

A. Either obsessions or compulsions:

Obsessions as defined by (1), (2), (3), and (4):

(1) recurrent and persistent thoughts, impulses, or images that are experienced, at some time during the disturbance, as intrusive and inappropriate and that cause marked anxiety or distress

(2) the thoughts, impulses, or images are not simply excessive worries about real-life problems

(3) the person attempts to ignore or suppress such thoughts, impulses, or images, or to neutralize them with some other thought or action

(4) the person recognizes that the obsessional thoughts, impulses, or images are a product of his or her own mind (not imposed from without, as in thought insertion)

Compulsions as defined by (1) and (2)

(1) repetitive behaviors (e.g., hand washing, ordering, checking) or mental acts (e.g., praying, counting, repeating words silently) that the person feels driven to perform in response to an obsession, or according to rules that must be applied rigidly

(2) the behaviors or mental acts are aimed at preventing or reducing distress or preventing some dreaded event or situation; however, these behaviors or mental acts either are not connected in a realistic way with what they are designed to neutralize or prevent or are clearly excessive

B. At some point during the course of the disorder, the person has recognized that the obsession or compulsion are excessive or unreasonable. Note: This does not apply to children

C. The obsessions or compulsions cause marked distress, are time consuming (take more than 1 hour a day), or significantly interfere with the person's normal route, occupation or academic functioning, or usual social activities or relationships

D. If another Axis I disorder is present, the content of the obsessions or compulsions is not restricted to it (e.g., preoccupations with food in presence of an eating disorder)

E. The disturbance is not due to the direct physiological effects of a substance (e.g., drug abuse, a medication) or a general medical condition

Appendix E

DIAGNOSTIC CRITERIA FOR TOURETTE DISORDER

A. Both multiple motor and one or more vocal tics have been present at some time during the illness, although not necessarily concurrently (a tic is a sudden, rapid, recurrent, nonrhythmic, stereotyped motor movement or vocalization)

B. The tics occur many times a day (usually in bouts) nearly every day or intermittently throughout a period of more than one year, and during this period there was never a tic-free period of more than three consecutive months

C. The disturbance causes marked distress or significant impairment in social, occupational, or other important areas of functioning

D. The onset is before age eighteen

E. The disturbance is not due to the direct physiological effects of substances (e.g., stimulants) or a general medical condition (e.g., Huntington's disease or postviral encephalitis)

Appendix F

Attention Deficit Disorders Association (ADDA)
P.O. Box 488
West Newbury, MA 01985
1-800-487-2282

Children with Attention Deficit Disorders (CHADD)
499 N.W. 70th Avenue, Suite 308
Plantation, FL 33317
(305) 587-3700
FAX (305) 587-4599

Learning Disabilities Association of America (LDA)
4156 Library Road
Pittsburgh, PA 15234
(412) 341-1515

National Center for Learning Disabilities (NCLD)
381 Park Avenue S., Suite 1420
New York, New York 10016
(212) 545-7510

Tourette Syndrome Association (TSA)
42-40 Bell Boulevard
Bayside, NY 11361
(718) 224-2999

Orton Dyslexia Society
8600 La Salle Road
Chester Building, Suite 382
Baltimore, MD 21286
(410) 296-0232

United States Department of Education
Office of Special Education and Rehabilitative Services
400 Maryland Ave. SW
Washington, DC 20202-2500
1-800-688-9889

United States Department of Education
Office of Civil Rights
400 Maryland Ave. SW
Washington, DC 20202-4135
(312) 353-6874

National Clearinghouse for Alcohol and
Drug Information
Department PP
P.O. Box 2345
Rockville, MD 20847-2345

Quest International
537 Jones Road
P.O. Box 566
Granville, OH 43023-0566
(614) 587-2800

Note: Many of these organizations have local or regional chapters
across the United States. Contact the organization to get information
about a chapter near your home. If no chapter is close to you, many
of the groups mentioned above will give you information about how
to begin a new chapter in your area.

Appendix G

MEDICATIONS COMMONLY PRESCRIBED
TO IMPROVE BEHAVIOR, MOOD, AND LEARNING

CATEGORY	MEDICATIONS	+THERAPEUTIC EFFECTS AND −SIDE EFFECTS
Psychostimulants	Methylphenidate HCl (Ritalin) Dextroamphetamine Sulfate (Dexedrine) Pemoline (Cylert)	+ May reduce impulsivity, increase attentional strength, diminish motor activity, enhance certain memory functions. − May cause tics, loss of appetite, growth delays, sleep problems, personality change; Premoline may disrupt liver function.
Tricyclic Antidepressants	Desipramine HCl (Norpramin, Pertofrane) Clomipramine HCl (Anafranil) Amitriptyline HCl (Elavil, Endep)	+ May reduce anxiety, depressive symptoms, aggression, overactivity, obsessive-compulsive signs. − May cause sedation, changes in heart rhythm, gastrointestinal disturbance.
Aminoketones	Bupropion HCl (Wellbutrin)	+ May reduce hyperactivity, anxiety, and aggressive tendencies. − May cause insomnia, headaches, gastrointestinal distress, seizures.
Lithium Preparations	Lithium Carbonate (Eskalith, Lithotabs)	+ May be effective in bipolar illness (manic-depression); may also help in depression when other drugs fail. − May cause gastrointestinal upset, tremor, weight gain, urinary symptoms, poor motor coordination.

CATEGORY	MEDICATIONS	+THERAPEUTIC EFFECTS AND –SIDE EFFECTS
Serotonin Re-uptake Inhibitors	Fluxetine HCl (Prozac) Sertraline HCl (Zoloft) Paroxetine HCl (Paxil)	+ May reduce anxiety, impulsivity, overactivity, obsessive-compulsive tendencies. – May worsen attention deficits, cause nervousness, result in oversedation.
Anti-psychotic	Haloperidol (Haldol)	+ May help attention in low doses, reduce tics in Tourette Syndrome, lessen aggressive symptoms. – May be overly sedative, interfere with cognition and learning, cause movement disorder (tardive dyskinesia).
Alpha-Adrenergic Agonists	Clonidine HCl (Catapres) Guanfacine HCl (Tenex)	+ May increase frustration tolerance, reduce impulsivity, improve task-oriented behaviors in children with, motoric overactivity, lessen tics in Tourette Syndrome, improve sleep. – May overly sedate, cause fall in blood pressure, induce depression or other mood disorder.

* ALL OF THESE MEDICATIONS HAVE ADDITIONAL, POSSIBLE EFFECTS, BOTH DETRIMENTAL AND BENEFI-CIAL. DIFFERENT CHILDREN ARE APT TO RESPOND OR REACT DIFFERENTLY TO THE SAME DRUG. THERE ARE SOME DIFFERENCES IN EFFECTS, SIDE EFFECTS, AND DURATIONS OF ACTION BETWEEN THE DRUGS WITHIN A SINGLE CATEGORY.

ALTHOUGH MUCH EXCELLENT RESEARCH ON THE USE OF THESE MEDICATIONS CONTINUES, SURPRIS-INGLY LITTLE IS ACTUALLY KNOWN ABOUT THEM. THEIR PRECISE DOSAGES, THEIR LONG-RANGE SIDE EFFECTS, AND USE IN VARIOUS COMBINATIONS REQUIRE FURTHER INVESTIGATION. FOR THIS REASON, WE SUGGEST A CONSERVATIVE APPROACH TO THEIR USE.

Source: Educational Care by Mel Levine, M.D.
Revised by Arnold Shapiro, M.D.

Appendix H

UNITED STATES DEPARTMENT OF EDUCATION
OFFICE OF SPECIAL EDUCATION AND REHABILITIVE SERVICES
THE ASSISTANT SECRETARY

MEMORANDUM

DATE :   Septmber 16, 1991

TO :   Chief State School Officers

FROM :   Robert R. Davila
            Assistant Secretary
            Office of Special Education and Rehabilitative Services

            Michael L. Williams
            Assistant Secretary
            Office for Civil Rights

            John T. MacDonald
            Assistant Secretary
            Office of Elementary and Secondary Education

SUBJECT: Clarification of Policy to Address the Needs of Children with
            Attention Deficit Disorders within General and/or Special Education

I. Introduction

There is a growing awareness in the education community that attention deficit disorder (ADD) and attention deficit hyperactive disorder (ADHD) can result in significant learning problems for children with those conditions.[1] While estimates of the
prevalence of ADD vary widely, we believe that three to five percent of school-aged
children may have significant educational problems related to this disorder. Because
ADD has broad implications for education as a whole, the Department believes it
should clarify State and local responsibility under Federal law for addressing the
needs of children with ADD in the schools. Ensuring that these students are able to

---

[1] While we recognize that the disorders ADD and ADHD vary, the term ADD is being used to encompass
children with both disorders.

reach their fullest potential is an inherent part of the National education goals and AMERICA 2000. The National goals, and the strategy for achieving them, are based on the assumptions that: (1) all children can learn and benefit from their education; and (2) the educational community must work to improve the learning opportunities for all children.

This memorandum clarifies the circumstances under which children with ADD are eligible for special education services under Part B of the Individuals with Disabilities Education Act (Part B), as well as the Part B requirements for evaluation of such children's unique educational needs. This memorandum will also clarify the responsibility of State and local educational agencies (SEAs and LEAs) to provide special education and related services to eligible children with ADD under Part B. Finally, this memorandum clarifies the responsibilities of LEAs to provide regular or special education and related aids and services to those children with ADD who are not eligible under Part B, but who fall within the definition of "handicapped person" under Section 504 of the Rehabilitation Act of 1973. Because of the overall educational responsibility to provide services for these children, it is important that general and special education coordinate their efforts.

II. Eligibility for Special Education and Related Services under Part B

Last year during the reauthorization of the Education of the Handicapped Act (now the Individuals with Disabilities Education Act), Congress gave serious consideration to including ADD in the definition of "children with disabilities" in the statute. The Department took the position that ADD does not need to be added as a separate disability category in the statutory definition since children with ADD who require special education and related services can meet the eligibility criteria for services under Part B. This continues to be the Department's position.

No change with respect to ADD was made by Congress in the statutory definition of "children with disabilities;" however, language was included in Section 102(a) of the Education of the Handicapped Act Amendments of 1990 that required the Secretary to issue a Notice of Inquiry (NOI) soliciting public comment on special education for children with ADD under Part B. In response to the NOI (published November 29, 1990 in the *Federal Register)*, the Department received over 2000 written comments, which have been transmitted to the Congress. Our review of these written comments indicates that there is confusion in the field regarding the extent to which children with ADD may be served in special education programs conducted under Part B.

A. Description of Part B

Part B requires SEAs and LEAs to make a free appropriate public education (FAPE) available to all eligible children with disabilities and to ensure that the rights and protections of Part B are extended to those children and their parents. 20 U.S.C.

1412(2); 34 CFR §§300.121 and 300.2. Under Part B, FAPE, among other elements, includes the provision of special education and related services, at no cost to parents, in conformity with an individualized education program (IEP). 34 CFR §300.4.

In order to be eligible under Part B, a child must be evaluated in accordance with 34 CFR §§300.530–300.534 as having one or more specified physical or mental impairments, and must be found to require special education and related services by reason of one or more of these impairments.[2] 20 U.S.C. 1401(a)(1); 34 CFR §300.5. SEAs and LEAs must ensure that children with ADD who are determined eligible for services under Part B receive special education and related services designed to meet their unique needs, including special education and related services needs arising from the ADD. A full continuum of placement alternatives, including the regular classroom, must be available for providing special education and related services required in the IEP.

B. Eligibility for Part B services under "Other Health Impaired" Category

The list of chronic or acute health problems included within the definition of "other health impaired" in the Part B regulations is not exhaustive. The term "Other health impaired" includes chronic or acute impairments that result in limited alertness, which adversely affects educational performance. Thus, children with ADD should be classified as eligible for services under the "other health impaired" category in instances where the ADD is a chronic or acute health problem that results in limited alertness, which adversely affects educational performance. In other words, children with ADD, where ADD is a chronic or acute health problem, resulting in limited alertness, may be considered disabled under Part B solely on the basis of this disorder with the "other health impaired" category in situations where special education and related services are needed because of the ADD.

C. Eligibility for Part B services under Other Disability Categories

Children with ADD are also eligible for services under Part B if the children satisfy the criteria applicable to other disability categories. For example, children with ADD are also eligible for services under the "specific learning disability" category of Part B if they meet the criteria stated in §§300.5(b)(9) and 300.541 or under the "seriously emotionally disturbed" category of Part B if they meet the criteria stated in §300.5(b)(8).

---

[2]The Part B regulations define 11 specified disabilities. 34 CFR §300.5(b)(1)–(11). The Education of the Handicapped Act Amendments of 1990 amended the Individuals with Disabilities Education Act [formerly the Education of the Handicapped Act] to specify that autism and traumatic brain injury are separate disability categories. *See* section 602(a)(1) of the Act, to be codified at 20 U.S.C. 1401(a)(1).

III. Evaluations under Part B

A. Requirements

SEAs and LEAs have an affirmative obligation to evaluate a child who is suspected of having a disability to determine the child's need for special education and related services. Under Part B, SEAs and LEAs are required to have procedures for locating, identifying, and evaluating all children who have a disability or are suspected of having a disability and are in need of special education and related services. 34 CFR §§300.128 and 300.220. This responsibility, known as "child find," is applicable to all children from birth through 21, regardless of the severity of their disability.

Consistent with this responsibility and the obligation to make FAPE available to all eligible children with disabilities, SEAs and LEAs must ensure that evaluations of children who are suspected of needing special education and related services are conducted without undue delay. 20 U.S.C. 1412(2). Because of its responsibility resulting from the FAPE and child find requirements of Part B, an LEA may not refuse to evaluate the possible need for special education and related services of a child with a prior medical diagnosis of ADD solely by reason of that medical diagnosis. However, a medical diagnosis of ADD alone is not sufficient to render a child eligible for services under Part B.

Under Part B, before any action is taken with respect to the initial placement of a child with a disability in a program providing special education and related services, "a full and individual evaluation of the child's educational needs must be conducted in accordance with requirements of §300.532." 34 CFR §300.531. Section 300.532(a) requires that a child's evaluation must be conducted by a multidisciplinary team, including at least one teacher or other specialist with knowledge in the area of suspected disability.

B. Disagreements over Evaluations

Any proposal or refusal of an agency to initiate or change the identification, evaluation, or educational placement of the child, or the provision of FAPE to the child is subject to the written prior notice requirements of 34 CFR §§300.504–300.505.[3] If a parent disagrees with the LEA's refusal to evaluate a child of the LEA's evaluation

---

[3]Section 300.505 of the Part B regulations sets out the elements that must be contained in the prior written notice to parents:
(1) A full explanation of all the procedural safeguards available to the parents under Subpart E;
(2) A description of the action proposed or refused by the agency, an explanation of why the agency proposes or refuses to take the action, and a description of any options the agency considered and the reasons why those options were rejected;
(3) A description of each evaluation procedure, test, record, or report the agency uses as a basis for the proposal or refusal; and
(4) A description of any other factors which are relevant to the agency's proposal or refusal.
34 # CFR §300.505(a)(1)–(4).

and determination that a child does not have a disability for which the child is eligible for services under Part B, the parent may request a due process hearing pursuant to 34 CFR §§300.506-300.513 of the Part B regulations.

IV. Obligations Under Section 504 of SEAs and LEAs to Children with ADD Found Not To Require Special Education and Related Services Under Part B

Even if a child with ADD is found not to be eligible for services under Part B, the requirements of Section 504 of the Rehabilitation Act of 1973 (Section 504) and its implementing regulation at 34 CFR Part 104 may be applicable. Section 504 prohibits discrimination on the basis of handicap by recipients of Federal funds. Since Section 504 is a civil rights law, rather than a funding law, its requirements are framed in different terms than those of Part B. While the Section 504 regulation was written with an eye to consistency with Part B, it is more general, and there are some differences arising from the differing natures of the two laws. For instance, the protections of Section 504 extend to some children who do not fall within the disability categories specified in Part B.

A. Definition

Section 504 requires every recipient that operates a public elementary or secondary education program to address the needs of children who are considered "handicapped persons" under Section 504 as adequately as the needs of nonhandicapped persons are met. "Handicapped person" is defined in the Section 504 regulation as any person who has a physical or mental impairment which substantially limits a major life activity (e.g., learning). 34 CFR §104.3(j). Thus, depending on the severity of their condition, children with ADD *may* fit within that definition.

B. Programs and Services Under Section 504

Under Section 504, an LEA must provide a free appropriate public education to each qualified handicapped child. A free appropriate public education, under Section 504, consists of regular or special education and related aids and services that are designed to meet the individual student's needs and based on adherence to the regulatory requirements on educational setting, evaluation, placement, and procedural safeguards. 34 CFR §§104.33, 104.34, 104.35, and 104.36. A student may be handicapped within the meaning of Section 504, and therefore entitled to regular or special education and related aids and services under the Section 504 regulation, even though the student may not be eligible for special education and related services under Part B.

Under Section 504, if parents believe that their child is handicapped by ADD, the LEA must evaluate the child to determine whether he or she is handicapped as defined by Section 504. If an LEA determines that a child is not handicapped under Section 504, the parent has the right to contest that determination. If the child is determined to be handicapped under Section 504, the LEA must make an individualized determination of the child's educational needs for regular or special education or related aids and services. 34 CFR §104.35. For children determined to be handicapped under Section 504, implementation of an individualized education program developed in accordance with Part B, although not required, is one means of meeting the free appropriate public education requirements of Section 504.[4] The child's education must be provided in the regular education classroom unless it is demonstrated that education in the regular environment with the use of supplementary aids and services cannot be achieved satisfactorily. 34 CFR §104.34.

Should it be determined that the child with ADD is handicapped for purposes of Section 504 and needs only adjustments in the regular classroom, rather than special education, those adjustments are required by Section 504. A range of strategies is available to meet the educational needs of children with ADD. Regular classroom teachers are important in identifying the appropriate educational adaptions and interventions for many children with ADD.

SEAs and LEAs should take the necessary steps to promote coordination between special and regular education programs. Steps also should be taken to train regular education teachers and other personnel to develop their awareness about ADD and its manifestations and the adaptations that can be implemented in regular education programs to address the instructional needs of these children. Examples of adaptations in regular education programs could include the following:

> providing a structured learning environment; repeating and simplifying instructions about in-class and homework assignments; supplementing verbal instructions with visual instructions; using behavioral management techniques; adjusting class schedules; modifying test delivery; using tape recorders, computer-aided instruction, and other audio-visual equipment; selecting modified textbooks or workbooks; and tailoring homework assignments.

Other provisions range from consultation to special resources and may include reducing class size; use of one-on-one tutorials; classroom aides and note takers; involvement of a "services coordinator" to oversee implementation of special programs and services, and possible modification of nonacademic times such as lunchroom, recess, and physical education.

Through the use of appropriate adaptations and interventions, in regular classes, many of which may be required by Section 504, the Department believes that LEAs will be able to effectively address the instructional needs of many children with ADD.

C. Procedural Safeguards Under Section 504

Procedural safeguards under the Section 504 regulation are stated more generally than in Part B. The Section 504 regulation requires the LEA to make available a sys-

---

[4]Many LEAs use the same process for determining the needs of students under Section 504 that they use for implementing Part B.

tem of procedural safeguards that permits parents to challenge actions regarding the identification, evaluation, or educational placement of their handicapped child whom they believe needs special education or related services. 34 CFR §104.36. The Section 504 regulation requires that the system of procedural safeguards include notice, an opportunity for the parents or guardian to examine relevant records, an impartial hearing with opportunity for participation by the parents or guardian and representation by counsel, and a review procedure. Compliance with procedural safeguards of Part B is one means of fulfilling the Section 504 requirement.[5] However, in an impartial due process hearing raising issues under the Section 504 regulation, the impartial hearing officer must make a determination based upon that regulation.

V. Conclusion

Congress and the Department have recognized the need to provide information and assistance to teachers, administrators, parents and other interested persons regarding the identification, evaluation, and instructional needs of children with ADD. The Department has formed a work group to explore strategies across principal offices to address this issue. The work group also plans to identify some ways that the Department can work with the education associations to cooperatively consider the programs and services needed by children with ADD across special and regular education.

In fiscal year 1991, the Congress appropriated funds for the Department to synthesize and disseminate current knowledge related to ADD. Four centers will be established in Fall, 1991 to analyze and synthesize the current research literature on ADD relating to identification, assessment, and interventions. Research syntheses will be prepared in formats suitable for educators, parents and researchers. Existing clearinghouses and networks, as well as Federal, State, and local organizations will be utilized to disseminate these research syntheses to parents, educators and administrators, and other interested persons.

In addition, the Federal Resource Center will work with SEAs and the six regional resource centers authorized under the Individuals with Disabilities Education Act to identify effective identification and assessment procedures, as well as intervention strategies being implemented across the country for children with ADD. A document describing current practice will be developed and disseminated to parents, educators and administrators, and other interested persons through the regional resource centers network, as well as by parent training centers, other parent and consumer organizations, and professional organizations. Also, the Office for Civil Rights' ten regional offices stand ready to provide technical assistance to parents and educators.

It is our hope that the above information will be of assistance to your State as you plan for the needs of children with ADD who require special education and re-

---

[5]Again, many LEAs and some SEAs are conserving time and resources by using the same due process procedures for resolving disputes under both laws.

lated services under Part B, as well as for the needs of the broader group of children with ADD who do not qualify for special education and related services under Part B, but for whom special education or adaptations in regular education programs are needed. If you need to ask any questions, please contact Jean Peelen, Office for Civil Rights; (Phone: 202/732-1635), Judy Schrag, Office of Special Education Programs (Phone: 202/732-1007); or Dan Bonner, Office of Elementary and Secondary Education (Phone: 202/401-0984).

Extra Forms

Children change often. Be sure to keep your child's symptoms and strengths sheet up to date.

Your Child's Symptoms and Strengths

ADD Symptoms	Strengths

When problem situations arise use your child's personal worksheet to take a critical look at the cause and possible solutions.

Your Child's Personal Worksheet

Name two situations causing problems or tension in school.

1. _____

   _____

2. _____

   _____

How is ADD related to these problems? What symptoms do you see described?

Pick several strengths that could be used to overcome or bypass the above problems. Consider the interventions. Which would be appropriate, considering your child's strengths?

Home-School Communication

CHILD'S NAME: DATE:

TEACHER'S NAME:

Goals	MON.	TUE.	WED.	THUR.	FRI.
1. Assignments turned in					
2. In class on time					
3. Asked questions on topic					

Comments:

key: I = Improvement seen
      N = No improvement

Glossary

Alphabet soup: The name changes ADD has undergone over the past one hundred years.

Attention Deficit/Hyperactivity Disorder, Predominantly Inattentive Type: Having only met the DSM-IV criteria for inattention.

Attention Deficit/Hyperactivity Disorder, Predominantly Hyperactive/ Impulsive Type: Having met only the DSM- IV criteria for hyperactivity- impulsivity.

Attention Deficit/Hyperactivity Disorder, Combined Type: Having met both the DSM-IV criteria for inattention and hyperactivity- impulsivity.

Bypass strategies: The skills children develop that use their strengths to overcome or go around their weaknesses and deficits.

CHADD: A national parents' support group with regional chapters. (See appendix for information about a chapter in your area.)

Comorbid disorders: Disorders often diagnosed along with ADD. Included might be Tourette syndrome, learning disabilities, obsessive compulsive disorder, oppositional defiant disorder, conduct disorder, depression, sensory integration issues, and language processing disabilities.

Demystification: Removing the mystery by learning the facts through education.

DSM IV: A manual compiled by the American Psychiatric Association (APA). Provides the criteria for the diagnosis of AD/HD, along with other disorders.

Dyscalculia: "Teacher talk" to describe difficulty with mathematics.

Dysgraphia: "Teacher talk" to describe difficulty with the writing process.

Dyslexia: "Teacher talk" to describe difficulty with reading.

Expressive language: Making an appropriate response either orally or written.

FM voice: A soft monotone voice used over and over to hypnotize the child or professional into seeing things from your perspective.

Fine motor: The use of the smaller muscles to complete more precise movements such as handwriting and coloring within the lines.

504 Plan: A plan of action written by the parents and school to address the specific needs of the child diagnosed with ADD/ADHD whose rights are protected under Section 504 of the Rehabilition Act of 1973.

Gross motor: The use of the body's larger muscles to coordinate such movements as running, skipping, swimming.

Hyperactivity: The body, even without batteries, that keeps going and going. A body in perpetual motion.

"I" message: A nonjudgmental way of communicating your feelings about a behavior or situation.

Impulsivity: Leaping before looking. Acting before thinking through the consequences of those actions.

Inattention: Having a head on a swivel. Attends to everything and has difficulty with selective attending.

Individual Education Plan (IEP): A plan of action written by parents and school for the child with learning disabilities.

Intervention Assistance Team (IAT): A problem-solving process to address the needs of children at risk within the classroom.

Invisible Disorder: Another way of describing ADD because there are no visible signs of the disorder.

Labels: Terms used to identify children's learning difficulties or ADD symptoms. They are useful in accessing services, but should be used with caution in order to avoid harming the child's spirit.

Mind journeys: Daydreaming or free flight of ideas. A linking of thoughts that distracts an individual's attention.

Neurotransmitters: Chemicals produced by the brain that pass along messages.

Nonverbal language: Language that is unspoken. Gestures, posture, and facial expressions are examples of how we use the body to communicate.

Pragmatic language: Conversational language that uses words and the body to communicate.

Psychiatrist: A medical doctor who can diagnose for ADD, provide therapy, and administer and monitor medication.

Psychologist: Usually has a Ph.D. Can provide a diagnosis and therapy but cannot prescribe medication.

Receptive language: Making sense of what is being said.

Red flags: Behaviors or statements warning parents and professionals that intervention may be needed.

Reticular formation: The brain's filtering system.

Self-monitoring: The child's ability to be aware of his actions and make corrections when appropriate. For example, responding to the STAR concept or checking back over math problems or test answers for omissions or errors.

SPECT Scans: Tests using computer technology to locate "hot spots" within the brain.

Spectrum of ADD: A visual way of indicating the intensity of the ADD and related disorders. It ranges from mild to severe.

Social register: Matching what is said to the person receiving the message. Street language with peers and a more formal language with adults.

Social skills: Knowing what actions are appropriate to fit the situation presented.

STAR: A visual reminder to help manage impulsivity.

Strengths: Hobbies, interests, or talents a person possesses that may be used to compensate for problematic symptoms of ADD.

Tag-team parenting: When parents take turns working with their child. As each parent is on the verge of burnout, one parent jumps in and takes the majority of responsibility for the child while the other parent takes a well-deserved rest.

Teacher talk: The jargon or educational terms teachers use that may be confusing to parents.

Time out: A quiet place to calm down and regain control. May be used by parent or child.

Tourette syndrome: A disorder often diagnosed with ADD. Most commonly identified by motor and vocal tics.

Whirlwind: An often misunderstood person with many talents and hidden strengths.

Wide umbrella of disorders: A way of describing ADD and all the disorders and manifestations related to it.

Bibliography

Amen, Daniel G., M.D. *Images of the Mind* (Fairfield, Calif.: Mind Works Press, 1995).

American Psychiatric Association. *Diagnostic and Statictical Manual of Mental Disorders* (Washington, D.C., 1994).

Bennis, Warren G., Kenneth D. Benne, and Robert Chin. *The Planning of Change* (New York: Holt, Reinholdt, & Winston, 1985).

Borba, Michele. *Esteem Builders: A Self-Esteem Curriculum for Improving Student Achievement, Behavior, and School Climate* (Rolling Hills Estates, Calif.: Jalmar Press, 1989).

Comings, David E. *Tourette Syndrome and Human Behavior* (Duarte, Calif.: Hope Press, 1990).

Department of Education, Division of Elementary and Secondary Education. *Intervention Assistance Team Models: Sharing the Responsibility for Success* (Columbus, Ohio, 1988).

Dryfoos, Joy G. *Adolescents at Risk: Prevalence and Prevention* (New York: Oxford University Press, 1990).

Goperude, Eric N. *OSAP Prevention Monograph Preventing Adolescent Drug Use: From Theory to Practice* (Rockville, Md.: U.S. Department of Health and Human Services Public Health Service Alcohol, Drug Abuse, and Mental Health Administration, 1991).

Gordon, Michael. *I Would if I Could* (DeWitt, N.Y.: GSI Publications, 1993).

———. *My Brother's a World-Class Pain: A Sibling's Guide to ADHD* (DeWitt, N.Y.: GSI Publications, 1992).

———. *Jumpin' Johnny Get Back to Work* (DeWitt, N.Y.: GSI Publications, 1991)

Hallowell, Edward M., MD, and Ratey, John J., M.D. *Driven to Distraction* (New York: Pantheon Books, 1994)

Hauser, Peter, M.D., et al. "Attention Deficit-Hyperactivity Disorder in People with Generalized Resistance to Thyroid Hormone" (*The New England Journal of Medicine* 328: 997–1001).

Kelley, Mary Lou. *School-Home Notes: Promoting Children's Classroom Success* (New York: Guildford Press, 1990).

Knighton, Art. "Human Behavior in the Social Environment (class lecture at the University of Cincinnati School of Social Work, Cincinnati, July 1995).

Lab, Steven, and John T. Whitehead. *Juvenile Justice* (Cincinnati: Anderson Publishing Company, 1990).

Levine, Melvin, M.D. *All Kinds of Minds* (Cambridge, Mass.: Educator's Publishing Service, Inc., 1993).

———. *Keeping a Head in School* (Cambridge, Mass.: Educator's Publishing Service, Inc., 1990).

———. *Educational Care* (Cambridge, Mass.: Educator's Publishing Service, Inc., 1994).

Miller, Sherod, Daniel Wackman, Elam Nunnally, and Phyllis Miller. *Connecting with Self and Others* (Littleton, Colo.: Interperson Communications Programs, Inc., 1988).

Quinn, Patricia O., M.D. *ADD and the College Student* (New York: Magination Press, 1994).

Quinn, Patricia O., M.D., and Judith M. Stern. *Putting on the Brakes: Young People's Guide to Understanding Attention Deficit Hyperactivity Disorder* (New York: Magination Press, 1991).

Still, G.F., M.D. "Some Abnormal Psychical Conditions in Children" (*Lancet* i: 1008–1012, 1077–1082, 1163–1168, 1902).

Weiss, Gabrielle, and Lily Trokenberg Hechtman. *Hyperactive Children Grown Up* (New York: Guildford Press, 1986).

Williford, Steve. *The Longaberger Story and How We Did It* (New York: The Lincoln-Bradley Publishing Group, 1991).

Wolraich, Mark L., M.D., et al. "Effects of Diets High in Sucrose or Aspartame on the Behavior and Cognitive Performance of Children" (*The New England Journal of Medicine* 330: 301–307, 1994).

Zametkin, Alan J., M.D., et al. "Cerebral glucose metabolism in Adults with Hyperactivity of Childhood Onset" (*The New England Journal of Medicine* 323: 1361–1366, 1990).

————. "Attention-Deficit Disorder: Born to Be Hyperactive?" (*The Journal of the American Medical Association* 273: 1871–1874, 1955).

Zins, J.E., et al. *Helping Students Succeed in the Regular Classroom* (San Francisco: Jossey-Bass Publishers, 1988).

Songs

Bradock, Bobby. "Small Y'all." *Randy Travis This Is Me* (Sunny Tree Publishing Co., Inc., BMI, Warner Bros. Records Inc., 1994).

Black, Jeff. "That's Just About Right." *Blackhawk* (Warner-Tamberlane Publishing Corp, BMI, Arista Records, 1994).

Carpenter, Mary Chapin. "Why Walk When You Can Fly." *Stones in the Road* (Why Walk Music, Sony Music Entertainment, 1994).

Jennings, Greg, Van Stephenson, Henry Paul. "Let 'em Whirl." *Blackhawk* (EMI Blackwood Music, Inc., Warner Tamberlane Publishing Corp, BMI, Greg Jennings Music (ASCAP), Arista Records, 1994).

Videos

Goldstein, Sam. *Why Won't My Child Pay Attention?* (1989).

Lavoie, Richard. *Last One Picked, First One Picked On* (1994).

Index